SURVIVING IN SALES IN CORPORATE AMERICA

DOUGLAS DILLEY

SURVIVING IN SALES IN CORPORATE AMERICA

CONTENTS

First View

We all look at where we are and on occasions ask, "How did I end up in this profession?". As we followed this path of life, encountering many turns and bumps, we make decisions that direct us toward our current occupations. I was working the inside operations for a very small company, performing functions such as shipping and receiving, order processing, inventory control and handling incoming phone calls. I convinced the owner to let me try my hand out in the marketplace - setting up distributors in different parts of the country that had no representation of our products. Every time I ventured out into the market, I would return with orders and/or a new distributor. Soon after the company was sold, my new boss said I had two weeks left working in the office and then I would be made a fulltime outside salesperson. That was a very long time ago and I have been an outside salesperson ever since.

So after more than thirty-five years in the selling profession, I thought I would take some time and reflect on this journey. Selling is a subject that seems to have been with us since man first tried to convince others to conform and accept. Whether it be to different philosophic states of thinking such as a different religious or political view, or to purchase. An occurrence happens when changing a person's decision process, creating a different state of being, a different state of mind.

As a child, convincing your peers to partake in an activity would be an example of selling. Being the loudest, the tallest, the strongest, using physical traits to sway others to participate in chosen activities such as a television show, a video game, or a sporting activity is an act of selling. To convince someone to purchase your products is to create a trust between a seller and a buyer that can provide economic rewards and secure enjoyment. Discussions of whats, whys and outcomes develop rapport, connections, conversational exchanges and presenting the pros and cons. Questions arise such as: "Would my parents approve?" or "Would my parents care one way or the other?". What is the cost of the outcome - a punishment or a reward?

First encounters with another group or person sets the stage for a future relationship. A person carries all their baggage of personalities and emotions. Sometimes there are personality clashes and sometimes not, but a smile and a sense of sincerity can set the stage for a receptive meeting.

I believe we all want to be liked, understood, and listened to with respect, but we need to remember to reciprocate. An exchange of ideas, stories, information, and history can build rapport and develop respect.

To receive respect, one needs to give respect. How do we give respect? I try to be as polite as possible, use good manners, and give your counterpart time to express him/herself. Do not interrupt, listen carefully during conversations, empathize and try to be understanding and gracious, thanking them for their time. As time passes, your customers will start greeting you as a friend - and doing business with friends will give you a feeling of accomplishment which goes beyond the monetary rewards.

From my business law class in college, the old "Offer and Acceptance" rule has always lingered with me. You offer your time, services, or products, but in order to consummate a sale there must be an acceptance. That acceptance needs to be some type of legal document such as a purchase order or signed agreement. This will give the seller and buyer a guideline on what is expected of each other. What the sale includes and what is not included should be documented so if situations arise that are outside the scope of the agreement document, they can be addressed separately from the original idea of what was covered.

You are a product of your past with all the decisions you have made as you faced the many forks in the road of life. My father was a purchasing agent for the largest aluminum producer (Alcoa) for over 38 years. Therefore, I am a salesperson raised by a professional buyer of a major corporation. I believe that gave me a good foundation to become a professional salesperson. Throughout my career experiences, with all the successful and disappointing times that the occupation had to offer, the rewards far outnumbered the disappointments. The reward of acceptance, of a yes, and a signed agreement or purchase order to proceed is well worth the time and effort of building a relationship with a customer.

After all those years in the selling profession I have finally retired. How I got into this occupation is somewhat of a common occurrence. Just like everyone else going through life, we find ourselves in our own occupations and careers.

My father and mother grew up in the 1930s during the great depression. My father was born in 1920 to a Longshoreman. His mother was a World War One bride brought to Oregon from Liverpool, England. They settled in Portland, Oregon where my grandfather provided security for the family. When the economic depression occurred during the 1930s my grandfather lost his job along with his home and moved across the Columbia River to Vancouver, Washington. To provide for his family, my grandfather did odd jobs cutting cord wood for 50 cents per cord (a cord of wood is 4x4x8 feet!), finally working river side docks in the grain elevators filling ships for export.

Prior to World War Two my father helped with the construction of the local Alcoa Aluminum manufacturing plant and then went on to school at Washington State University. During his second year at school on December 7, 1940, Japan attacked Pearl Harbor. Americans across the country enlisted into the military to defend our country. My father joined the US Navy and served in the Pacific for the duration of the war.

During high school my mother and father met each other and when my father was on leave from the war, they married. Upon his return from the war, they started their family. Having experienced different business ventures such as a typewriter and a Fuller Brush salesman, and because he had some college education along with managing on on-shore supplies warehouse for the Naval ships during the war, he was then hired back by the Alcoa aluminum plant as a Storeroom Manager handling the inventory to keep the plant operational. As his career progressed, he got involved with purchasing contracts, and all the necessary components and services to keep the plant functioning profitably. His responsibilities increased to a level where upper management was sending him to their facilities across the country and their mines in Africa to perform audits for profitability analysis. Once he was even sent to Washington, D.C. as a lobbyist. As a young man he also experienced manual labor while doing construction work for the Bonneville Dam on the Columbia River. Before I was born my father even built the house I grew up in. My mother lived there until she was 94 years old.

Like so many children who grew up during the great depression of the 1930s, my parents instilled in me a strong work ethic and the idea of saving your money and not spending it on foolish things.

There was a large local farmer who employed the children and teenagers during harvest time to pick the strawberry crop. So, at ten years old, I started picking strawberries and later pole beans, blueberries, and even red pie cherries. My father, who was not able to finish his college education at WSU, wanted all his children to be college educated

- so I saved every dollar I earned. I started my first savings account at the age of five. By the time I graduated from high school I was able to pay for all my college education at WSU. During those summers working on the farm I moved irrigation pipes, bucked hay bales, drove tractor, and other summers I worked as construction labor, a garbage man, and a railroad laborer. During the years at WSU I worked in campus kitchens for food and spending money.

I graduated in four years with a Bachelor of Arts in English Literature degree focusing on creative writing, and my grades were above average. During my college time I met some amazing people and to this day I have kept in touch with many of them. I enjoyed all types of people but always gravitated toward the literary arts. My parents were so happy and proud that I graduated! Because I paid for my college education on my own, for graduation my parents were able to present me with a round trip airline ticket to London. They thought I was going to be gone for about six to eight weeks, but I was gone for almost a year - traveling through Europe, Scandinavia, and Russia, living on the island of Ibiza, Spain, working for the Bulova Watch Company in Switzerland, and finally in Liverpool working as a waiter. I always tried to manage my money carefully so after my travels, I returned to work that summer at the local gas station, and that Fall I returned to WSU to study business.

During the late seventies and early eighties, I worked at industrial supply companies providing items and services such as bearings, conveyor belt systems, industrial hose products, fittings, working in the warehouse, shipping and receiving, inventory control and driving truck deliveries. A placement company connected me with a new startup company importing industrial pressure gauges and automotive gauges from Germany. I was hired to work the phone, perform inventory, and fill orders for shipment. It was then I first had the opportunity to sell in the outside market. At my previous jobs I kept seeing these salespeople dressed nicely, coming and going as they pleased, and they all seemed to have so much freedom. That is when I started thinking that these sales-people had it pretty good and I felt I could do what they do - sell. Then one day I came to work, and the owner of the company informed me that he had sold the company to an industrial hose supply company. On the first day my new boss walked through the door and informed me that I would be their new outside salesperson promoting the products and services of the company they had just purchased.

Well, it worked out great! Every time I went out into the field selling, I came back with orders. Then I started selling their whole product line. The company employed about ten people. It was a wonderful time - poker games at lunch and after work, and a keg of beer in the warehouse! This was the early eighties and some of my customers drank at lunch time. Today this would happen very rarely! There was only one problem - the company's owner did not believe in any form of commission for his salespeople. My sales were growing at a steady rate while my income was stagnated. Also, at the same time my wife and I had a mortgage and a new baby boy.

I had developed some good relationships and was becoming known in the business community. Then one day I had an offer to sell for one of the top industrial instrumentation supply companies in the North-west. I took their offer. I went from a straight salary company to my new employer as a straight commission salesperson for the first time. Within three years I tripled my income. During this time our second son arrived. I spent four years with this company. The owners kept the commission payment calculation very simple. As a salesperson you oversaw the amount of profit you generate from each sale. The profit was split three ways: one third went to the company, one third went to running the company, and one third was the salesperson's commission.

One day I was calling on one of my customers who was a world leader in the air conditioning industry. It was the fall of 1985 and I had developed a good business relationship with one of their engineers.

Every time he sold an energy retrofit on one of their large commercial air conditioning units, I would sell him all the automatic 3-way diverting actuating valves, pressure gauges, temperature gauges and switches. A year later they hired me as their salesperson. That was November 2, 1986, and we parted our relationship twenty-four years later. During those twenty-four years I learned the art of selling the best I could. There was not a day that went by without some type of learning experience. Such is life!

The following is an accumulation of selling encounters, advice, techniques, and business episodes that I hope you will enjoy and learn from.

CHAPTER 2

Remember Your First Sale

When I think of my career in sales, memories of my first selling experiences reappear and then I start thinking of how my parents raised me. What were their backgrounds that produced a child who became a professional salesperson? Some people say that you are a product of all your past experiences. If this is so, I am sure there were many experiences that helped me become a successful salesperson. However, you can determine the definition of success.

Both my parents grew up during the Great Depression of the 1930s, so my upbringing was based on hard work and saving money. In my case it was all about saving for your college education which equated to giving yourself a better chance and opportunity for a higher income level. We raised chickens for their eggs and for an occasional chicken dinner, and every summer I spent time weeding our vegetable garden.

My grandparents had a couple of large holly trees in their front yard. Every year around the first of December my father would fill the trunk of his car with clippings from those two holly trees. My older sister and brother and I would then select the best cuttings of branches with the reddest berries and fill our pull wagon with those clippings. Then the three of us would go door to door throughout the neighborhood selling holly clippings to the housewives for decorating for the Christmas season. I remember selling the small cuttings for 10 cents each and the larger ones for 25 or 50 cents each. Sometimes I would have discussions with the customers over pricing concerning quantity and quality of the clippings. These conversations were possibly my first negotiated sales.

Since I was the youngest, my older brother and sister would always send me to the front doors to confront prospects for our holly. Looking back today, I can only imagine the surprise of the adult opening their front door to a five-year-old little boy bundled up for the December weather saying, "Would you like to buy some holly for Christmas decorating?" We did quite well with our little enterprise, raising enough money to buy family Christmas presents. Of course, I think my father split the money up between the three of us. As I got older, I took the holly enterprise over and mounted cardboard boxes on my bicycle, filling them with Christmas holly. By using my bike, I could cover a larger territory and therefore increased my earnings.

Once a year during the last two weeks of August our family would travel to the mouth of the Columbia River and set up a camp with other families from our neighborhood and fish for the late summer Coho and Chinook salmon. I was not allowed to go salmon fishing until I was 10 years old. There were always many fishing boats at the boat ramp in the mornings heading out into the ocean and the mouth of the river in pursuit of salmon.

During those August days the children were left behind in camp. I would play all morning long exploring the driftwood beaches of Bakers Bay, building forts, playing tag, and fishing for bullheads and white suckers with the other children. My father taught my brother and I how to clean salmon at a very early age; I was so young I can't remember the first salmon I ever cleaned. One summer I found an old knife and started meeting the fishermen as their boats arrived at the shore, offering to clean their salmon for them. I charged 10 cents for the small ones and 25 cents for the larger salmon. The small salmon at the time were considered anything below 20 pounds. By the end of August, the boat ramp area smelled strongly of butchered salmon. That summer I made over $20. Not bad for a little boy running around the shoreline selling his services to clean salmon!

I believe these two examples of my childhood enterprises helped to mold my personality to approach people and provide a service or product they may need. Later in life I would do what is called today "cold call" selling - and I do not mean just calling up someone on the phone like a boiler room call center. A real cold call is going to a place of business unannounced, introducing yourself and discovering information that will assist you in obtaining a future business relationship. I really enjoyed cold call selling. My record for cold calls in one day was 19. To be successful, you must be respectful of the people you encounter in their business environments. This is the place they spend large amounts of their time - it is their home away from home.

So, from selling Christmas holly and cleaning salmon as a young boy, to later in life handling millions of dollars worth of contracts and product sales, I still used some of those introductions and closing techniques.

CHAPTER 3

Appearance Makes a Difference

It has been said that people make their judgement of a person during a first encounter within 30 seconds or less to determine if they like them and want to do business with them. Having the knowledge of this, your dress, personal hygiene, facial expressions and speaking ability all come into reference. If you smell bad, people will avoid you. If you are always frowning, you won't be as welcomed as a person smiling. Positive good energy attracts positive people. It was once said to me that people like doing business with people they like. Don't wear hats during a meeting - this is not polite or professional! Don't ever wear sunglasses, you want your customer to be able to look you in the eyes. It's been said that eyes are the window to the soul.

When calling on a place of business one should remember that you are a visitor, a guest - so politeness should be a necessity. The people you are visiting at this business establishment spend forty hours or more a week there. It is their home away from home. You are in their world, so be aware of this and be thankful for the fact that they are taking time from their workday to speak with you.

I sometimes mention the humorous fact that I was raised by a purchasing agent and became a salesperson because my father said that I would make a good salesman. He once told me that when a new salesperson entered his office, the first he did was look at their shoes. If the salesperson's shoes were not properly polished, their chance of doing business with him would be greatly diminished.

When greeting a receptionist, who is most likely the first person you will encounter when you enter a business, always try to have a pleasant smile on your face. Wait until the receptionist can acknowledge you. If you have an appointment already set up, that is best. If not, politely introduce yourself, stating who you are, who you represent and then ask who the best person is to speak with concerning your services. Sometimes you might be directed to a maintenance manager, the plant engineer, purchasing agent, or even the CEO or owner. You can ask the receptionist questions like: "Who is the purchasing agent?", "Who is the maintenance manager?", "What is the best way to contact that person?" and "When is the best time to connect with that person?". This gives the receptionist a feeling of power, which in fact they have. The receptionist is the gate keeper for their company, and they sometimes decide who gets to pass "go" and proceed into their company's environment. With certain companies you will need to pass a security background check, take safety training, or wear approved safety equipment.

Whether that first person you meet is a receptionist, a technician, janitor or maintenance manager, always be friendly and polite. These people may already, or in the future determine who will receive an order, issue purchase orders or review proposals. A salesperson is constantly being reviewed. Just like answering the telephone during your business day, sometimes you have no idea who you are speaking with. It could be your competitor trying to get information on your hourly labor rates, an owner of a major company checking your company out, or a potential customer wanting information that might determine what product or manufacturer to use on their next project. Once I was making sales calls on an international semiconductor company and developed a good relationship with the receptionist. By chance she had gone to high school with my older sister. Four years later that receptionist was the purchasing agent for that company and was issuing me orders for over $200,000.

A lot of the time we just don't know who we are speaking with. Therefore, it is best always to be kind and polite to whomever you may encounter and present yourself dressed properly, as if you truly want to do business.

CHAPTER 4

Be Creative

When you are out in the marketplace calling on perspective customers, the truth is you are just asking for the opportunity to prove yourself as a dependable person who delivers the goods on time with the best quality. Being creative can give you that unique edge and put you above your competitors. What you are trying to accomplish is to capture an order by your offer to provide a product or a service. Sometimes the customer's request comes when they ask for a quote or proposal. Once you receive their request, then you need to acquire as much information as possible to help you deliver the best proposal. This is the time to differentiate yourself from your competition by presenting a better delivery time or cost, to inform them that you have a local inventory, better trained service technicians and operational support personnel, better warranties, and quick response time to unscheduled service calls. You can also present references with testimonies from existing long-term customers to increase the customer's confidence in your company.

When it comes to pricing, calculate your cost and then determine what markup profit margin would best fit the sale. Of course, there are many times that the customer is very knowledgeable concerning the product and will require their own specifications to qualify and limit the number of competitors presenting proposals. This can be accomplished by their engineering specifications, defined emergency response time associated with penalties, or a required number of employees/technicians. There have been many times in my career when my relationship with a customer is so trusting that I was invited to assist in shaping the specifications of the RFP (Request for Proposal). This happens when a customer wishes to retain you and your company, or they wish to have your company as the new vendor of services and eliminate the competition. The ethics/human resource people would have a fit if they knew this was happening, but it occurs in the business world more than what you would think - over a lunch, a quick cup of coffee, at trade shows, association gatherings or behind closed doors.

I had an incident once where I was departing from a meeting with a customer, and he ran out into the parking lot to tell where my pricing needed to be to capture the order. Once I was competing with another manufacturer on a very large commercial air conditioning unit. I was on the phone with my customer trying to close the sale and I asked him how my price was looking. He hemmed and hawed a little and I started feeling somewhat negative about my asking price, so I dropped the price a few thousand dollars and asked him if that would put a smile on his face. He responded that it would! He purchased the equipment at that price, and I captured the order making a good profit margin. Plus, I sold him a multi-year maintenance program on the unit!

There always seems to be discussions in sales of where the sale price needs to be to win the order. Is it too high? Is there enough profit in the pricing to cover contingencies? Some pricing must be approved by management or the manufacturer you are representing due to the engineering specifications of the units.

There was a situation in San Francisco where two salesmen were working with a large customer who was about to purchase a large quantity of commercial air conditioning units. The pricing was nearly a million dollars and needed approval from the corporate office. One of the requirements was that the proposal needed to be delivered by 5pm on a given day. The proposal delivery day came and it was 4pm, and their corporate pricing people had not yet responded after multiple requests by the salesmen. So, they decided to place a blank line in the proposal where the price was supposed to appear and asked the customer to fill in the blank with their price for purchasing the units, then they would check with the factory to see if the customer's price was acceptable. When they received the proposal back from the customer with his price, they compared it to the approved factory price. The customer's fill price was much higher than the factory price! The customer was happy because he got to use his price, the salespeople were happy because the pricing created more commission and the factory was happy because the company would have a high profit margin on the manufacturing of units. Everyone was happy!

The lessons learned from these two stories is being creative and thinking outside the box can increase your sales. Also, ask the challenging questions that need to be asked such as, "How's my pricing look as compared to what you are seeing presently?". Creativity in selling will increase your sales along with your income.

CHAPTER 5

Be Aware How You Are Perceived

How your potential customers perceive you as a person is critical for developing relationships in the business community. All of us want to be accepted as good individuals, but the proof is in the pudding. If you want to be known as an honest, dependable person then you need to act like an honest, dependable person. If you want to be an organized person who can prioritize your business, then you should have a system to keep you organized helping prioritize your ever growing and changing business contacts.

Good salespeople have a sense of prioritizing their potential sales. The terms "keeping in touch", "following up" or "checking the status" with customers concerning a project or service are statements that can be used in the sales process. Sometimes the space of time between these initial contacts to perform a "trial close" can take only one follow up communication over a very short period, other times it takes a lengthy period of days, weeks, months or even years depending on the customer and their changing business situations.

A good salesperson must be aware of the fine line he balances between being obnoxious and being persistent. Sometimes it is like walking a tightrope; when should you call a customer to make that appointment? Sometimes, it is just best to ask when they would like to be contacted again concerning a future need. Sometimes, it is your gut feeling, your intuition. Usually the customer will tell you the timeline of the procurement; but to be on the safe side you need to ask these questions to receive the needed information:

"When do you plan on purchasing this equipment?"
"How will the project be phased in?"

You need this information so you can project your future sales. Delivery schedules can be very critical for the customer. Keeping the customer informed on the delivery of the products or services he has ordered is a way of building trust, loyalty and can strengthen your relationship by showing him you care about the business transaction and that you are a part of his team. You should always have a good reason for contacting your customer and you should state your reasons for doing so. Whether to gather more information or to provide helpful information such as confirming ship date and delivery or letting the customer know necessary adjustments have been made. Other times you can call your customer to see how things are going. You never know, he might have been transferred, promoted, or has passed away and there is a new person sitting in their chair who now makes the buying decisions.

Remember, your customer is usually terribly busy; respect their time. Get to the reason why you have contacted them. Make your emails short and to the point, easy to read and understandable. It is possible they may receive over 100 or more emails each day along with phone calls that are sometimes screened by his assistant, or his phone message inbox is full and they might only access it once a day. Emails and phone messages that drag on and on will usually get deleted quickly.

The sales tip here is to work at being perceived as a person who can get to the point of the matter while respecting their time, which gives you a better chance of closing more business.

CHAPTER 6

Always Address the Options

Do not forget to address all the options. Try to give your customer more than what they are requesting, but not too much. You don't want to bore them into trying to figure out what it all means. The customer might put the proposal aside because it is too timely to understand all the details and scope of services. I had customers more than once give me my competitors' proposals and ask if I could explain the content. This was a great feeling knowing my customer trusted me to decipher my competitors' proposals so they could explain it to their superior why they were keeping me as a provider of services.

At large Fortune 500 companies, they have teams of people that create the proposals for multi-million-dollar RFPs. They have teams of writers and reviewers and editors to create the final response proposal.

Some of these people have no sales experience and sometimes given very little time to focus 100% of their efforts to the task. When the proposal writer comes to the options section, they may decide that there is no need to present any options because they feel it is not required since they responded to all the customer's required specifications and requests. Usually, those companies lose the business to their competitors, because their competitors provide more services and products within the options section of the RFP, when the losing company failed to provide any optional services or products at all.

One morning while reading the daily newspaper, I came upon the comics section. One of the comics caught my attention. It was "Hagar the Terrible" showing the Vikings marching through the forest on their way to battle when the lead scout came across a broken arrow in the pathway. The little Viking scout brought the broken arrow to their leader exclaiming: "Captain, I found this broken arrow in the path. What does it mean?" Their leader thought for a moment and responded: "Low bidder got the contract." It struck me that so many times customers will take the lowest price and then later pay dearly to have the higher bidder return to correct the poor, shoddy service of the original low bidder. Always try to define precisely all your unique qualifications, look at all possible options for that product or service that might increase its quality, stressing that you may not be the lowest price but your services are of the highest standards as shown by references and qualifications.

Lesson learned - take into consideration the options you have available because your customers will get what they pay for and possibly in the long run may end up paying more.

CHAPTER 7

Use Your Personal Touch

When you give your proposals a personal creative touch, your customers will remember you when they sort through all the others they receive. This is another way of differentiating you from your competition. Delivery of a proposal can be done by email, US mail, and in person, sometimes with an on-the-spot discussion, or on a specific date and time in a sealed envelope that requires it to be stamped and dated with the time to verify that the proposal was delivered prior to the deadline for acceptance.

The US Postal Service once sent out a very large multi-million-dollar RFP. I believe it had something to do with an energy retrofit on many of their facilities across the country. A very well-known Fortune 500 company planned to respond to the RFP. They composed a team of professionals to work on the RFP. They worked on it for several weeks prior to the required delivery date. Finally, the proposal team had completed their reply to all the requirement and even presented optional services, special payment schedules, service delivery schedules with penalties for not meeting their stated schedules. The manager of the proposal, after having it approved for delivery by his supervisors, handed the proposal to the receptionist and told her: "Please send this out today."

When the US Postal Service representative received the proposal, he did not even bother to open it up, but instead threw it straight into the trash. The receptionist had shipped the proposal FedEx and the customer was the USPS. The manager should have instructed the receptionist to use the USPS carrier. Should the receptionist have known better? Sometimes it is the little simple things that make all the difference in the world. If your customer is the USPS, be darned sure you use them to ship your proposals! Think of all the cost that went into creating that proposal, all those people working long hours on that RFP. All that cost now shows up as a financial loss to the company - probably an exceptionally large dollar loss.

Early in my selling career I worked for a man who in his own right was a great salesman. One morning I was in the office when he was talking on the phone to one of his customers answering questions on products and filling out an order form. During the phone call he patiently answered questions from the caller, and they came to a decision over a pricing issue to close the sale. After the call was completed and he had hung up the phone he turned to me and said: "That guy just screwed me, but you know what? I will screw him twice as bad the next time and he will never know it." An old saying comes to mind with that event: "What goes around, comes around." We had sole distribution rights for the geographical region for that product the customer got such a great deal on and sooner or later he would have to come back to us to purchase more product - then he would pay a much higher price. This many was my boss for years. Whenever I started complaining about this or that customer situation that was preventing me from closing a sale or from making a critical contact he would always say: "Shut up and go sell." Which I usually did. Then one day while browsing through a bookstore I came across a book in the business section titled "Shut Up and Sell". Of course I purchased the book immediately. It was one of the best books on selling I ever read. Some of the best advice on selling

I learned came from that book. The advice was simple, but difficult to execute. I took away from that book two major rules in selling:

1. If you talk longer than 3 minutes with a decision maker, you might as well forget about leaving with an order or a signed contract in your hand. You have lost the advantage of creating a conversation, a relationship, or the ability to create a dialogue or rapport with your customer. Talk, listen, talk, listen, ask questions, make comments of something in his office that is connected to the customer. If you talk longer than 3 minutes, most likely you have lost the chance of closing the sale.
2. Once you ask for the order, shut up. Don't say another word. Your job is done, the ball is in his park now. It is time for the buyer to make the decision - approve the order or decline it. If questions arise, answer them and then be quiet.

I tried this technique after asking for an order once. I was in the buyer's office and said, "All I need now to proceed is a purchase order." and then I was quiet - I stopped talking. It felt uncomfortable and awkward, but I stayed silent. You may think you need to say more, explain more - you don't. You have already asked for the order. I sat there for an uncomfortable 3 to 5 minutes while the buyer shuffled papers and forms on his desk and took a phone call. Then out of the blue he reaches into his desk drawer and pulls out a purchase order, fills it out, signs it, and hands it to me. I thanked him and headed to my car. Mission accomplished.

I do realize that the five to seven figure dollar purchases take a long time to capture with multiple meeting, phone calls, accumulation of copious amounts of information being exchanged prior to the actual purchase order and multiple pricing approval meetings. Be aware of your competition and how you can differentiate yourself from them. Be creative, think outside the box, and what you can offer the customer that no one else is able to might make the difference in receiving the order or losing the order. Each sale is unique, and you need to adapt to each new situation. Attitude, a smile, being courteous, with good listening skills can give that slight advantage that can capture a new relationship and close more orders for you. Try to be unique, use your personal touch whenever you can, and you may see an increase in closing more sales.

CHAPTER 8

Follow the Requirements

Customers' requirements are critical when presenting your proposals. Always try to acquire all the possible needed information so your proposal addresses all their requirements. When a company or facility has a larger than normal project that needs to be addressed by an outside provider, they usually require the competing contractors to attend a mandatory walk through to personally view the condition, locational access of the project components to be addressed, and on-site meetings to answer any questions the bidding contractors may have and to confirm that tall the bidders understand what is required in presenting their proposals. The mandatory meeting or walk through gives the competitors the opportunity to see what is really involved, such as structural access, the need for rigging, requirements for electrical and mechanical services, to record model and serial numbers of the equipment to be addressed and questions.

There was an RFP at a state university concerning a rebuild of a large commercial mechanical air conditioning unit. In the university's bid package there was a date and time for a mandatory walk-through visit. I was scheduled to attend our annual regional sales meeting and could not make the walkthrough visit because of a company meeting out of town that same day. I had one of our technicians attend the walkthrough to represent our company so we could qualify as a bidder. The piece of equipment in question was manufactured by one of our competitors. I found out through my contact at the university that the salesperson had spent a tremendous amount of time with the university writing the specifications for the RFP. Therefore, they would be my main competition. When I returned from the regional sales meeting, I met with the technician to see who attended the walkthrough. He told me the bidding manufacturer did not have their factory service representative at the walkthrough. I immediately called the university's purchasing agent handling the RFP and asked him if the competing manufacturer would be disqualified from bidding the RFP because they did not attend the mandatory walkthrough. He said they were, in fact, disqualified for that reason. Later I found out that the competing salesperson felt he didn't need to attend the walkthrough because he wrote the specifications for the RFP. Arrogance cost him the chance to even bid the project. The technician also told me that there was only one other company besides us at the walkthrough, so my chances for capturing the project just then increased to 50%. However, I had no historical knowledge of how the unknown contractor may price the project. We priced the project at 35% profit margin, and our competitor was much higher. Though we didn't make as much profit as our competitor would have, we did receive the contract and obtained the profit we were asking to receive.

Learning from this experience, one must read the RFPs specifications carefully and make sure to attend all mandatory meetings and walkthroughs, and don't let your ego or arrogance cloud your vision.

CHAPTER 9

Don't Push the Envelope Too Hard

Good salespeople have a way of thinking creatively or "outside the box", using the rules to their advantage or pushing the limits to obtain new business. But you need to be careful and don't sacrifice your integrity by pushing the limits too far. If you push the envelope too hard, you will suffer the consequences.

A good friend of mine who sold for the same company as I did left our company for a regional sales manager position with one of our competitors in the Seattle market. When he departed our company, one of our best technicians went with him. His new company handled the Vancouver, B.C. region (VBC). While calling on the VBC territory a potential customer requested a bid on servicing several large air conditioning units that were manufactured by his old employer. My friend told his customer that his new company had a technician that was factory certified by his old employer's company. Once hearing this, the customer requested documentation showing the servicing technician had truly been certified and trained by the manufacture of the piece of the equipment to be serviced. This is when my friend pushed a little too hard on that envelope. He had some old letterhead from his old employer and fabricated a letter stating the technician was certified by that manufacturer to perform services on those particular air conditioning units, and back dated the letter to the time of his old employment. When the customer received the letter, he saw the address of the manufacturer's service office was in Seattle with their FAX number. So, he faxed the letter to the manufacturer's service office to verify the certification of the technician. When the service manager in the Seattle office received the 'false' certification letter with his old salesperson's signature on it, he immediately passed it on to his corporate headquarters legal department on the east coast who then contacted the company where my friend currently worked. A couple of months passed and on a Monday morning when my good friend went to his place of employment to start his work week, he was terminated on the spot without any notice.

You cannot use another company's letterhead to your advantage when you are not employed by them! The company whose letterhead was fraudulently used can take legal actions and the next thing you know you may find yourself in a room full of layers or in a court room. So, the upper management of the two companies came to an agreement just to terminate my friend rather than face a court case of fraudulent behavior. To this day that salesperson remains a good friend of mine and has become a very successful businessperson as president of a multi-million dollar company.

This story happened, and I am sure there are many situations similar to this one that have happened or are happening throughout the business world. Pushing the envelope sometimes works, but if you push too hard, it can cost you big. Sometimes you need to ask yourself if your actions might be considered illegal, or unethical in the eyes of the business consequences if you think you may be pushing too far.

CHAPTER 10

Dress to Sell

Dress yourself so you look presentable to the market in which you are selling. Over the years, dress and business has changed along with the market and culture. As I have mentioned previously, my father was a purchasing agent for Alcoa. I remember him every workday morning preparing himself for the day: clean shaven, white dress shirt and tie, slacks, matching sport coat and polished shoes. My mother kept all his white shirts and clacks washed, ironed and ready. As he departed he looked sharp and spotless, ready for his workday. He also expected the people he did business with the appear the same.

- <u>Semi-Conductor industry story</u>. I was calling on the Intel Corporation in Hillsboro, Oregon. I made the appointment with one of their process engineers. When I arrived for the meeting I was dressed in my normal attire at the time: white shirt and tie, matching slacks and sport coat, and shined dress shoes. I was dressed as how I thought a professional salesperson should be dressed. When the engineer arrived, he was wearing casual slacks, collared shirt, and comfortable walking shoes. I started thinking that I might be overdressed. The meeting went well, and I was able to set up a following presentation meeting for my products. Later that week having a conversation over lunch with a good business friend, we started talking about my appointment with Intel and doing business with them. That is when I learned that Intel had turned to a casual dress code, which at that time was quite new to the business world. When calling on this market you don't need to dress the white shirt/suit style and you cannot make assumptions as to whom you are speaking with - it could be the janitor, or the CEO.

- <u>Mirroring your market</u>. People feel more comfortable doing business and conversing with people who dress like they do. If you are doing business with farmers and you are selling John Deere tractors, you need to dress like a farmer. If you are selling to the logging industry, you need to dress like someone who has spent time in the woods harvesting timber. You don't want to look like a city slicker when selling to country folk and you don't want to dress like a person who looks like they just came in from the back 40 acres when dealing with the metropolitan market. Be cognizant of how your customers dress and you will have a better chance of creating a good business relationship with them.

Other times it may be better to be overdressed than underdressed. You never know where you will end up during the day. One moment you are in the basement of a dark, dingy mechanical room and the next you are in a conference room on the 42nd floor overlooking the city discussing a contract with a building owner. Every morning as you head off to work, look at yourself in the mirror and ask yourself, "Do I look like someone who others would want to do business with?" How you dress reflects who you are.

CHAPTER 11

Meeting Your Goals

Goal setting is important. Goals help you create a road map on where you want to be in the future. Setting goals drives you to become more competitive. When I first experienced commission selling, I had a couple of older bosses both around 25 years my senior. One was the owner of the company and the other was a regional manager. After about the first two years my customer base was increasing at a nice rate, and I was given a company car along with an expense account. Most of the company's accounts were large paper mills, chemical plants, and the semiconductor industry. My wife and I at the time had two infant boys. Being paid on commission, I received bi-monthly salary drawn against my commission pay and the commission that was greater than my salary draw was paid out quarterly. Therefore, at the beginning of every quarter it was a race to hit my salary draw against my commission (my break-even point) as quickly as possible. Once you hit your break-even number, the amount beyond that is "gravy". The learning lesson is: if you are not making your break-even mark in the first year or two of employment as a salesperson, you may want to start thinking of a change in your career.

At the time I was providing for four people along with a mortgage and waiting on my quarterly commission check starting to be financially stressful. My bi-weekly salary draw against my commission was becoming an economic strain - I was having trouble providing a comfortable living environment for my family between commission payouts. One morning prior to heading out to see my customers, I confronted the owner that I needed an increase in my bi-weekly salary draw to better provide for my family. His response was: "If you need more money, just go sell more." I said yes, I could do that, but waiting three months for a commission check put me in an uncomfortable financial position because my family expenses have increased. He said he would investigate my predicament and within ten minutes he returned with a nice salary draw increase which amounted to about a 20% increase. I would not have received that increased draw if I had not been bringing in enough profit to the company to cover that additional pay increase. The lesson here is that if you are increasing the profits for the company, the better the chance they will address your needs. If they don't, maybe it's time to take your services to another company who can compensate you properly.

I spent four very educational years at this company. We were an industrial instrumentation company representing manufacturers. Our product line was very impressive - process control valves for all types of applications, all kinds of flow meters, temperature and pressure instruments, metering pumps, and a valve and instrument repair facility.

Of course, all these products were developed and manufactured by companies who wanted their products promoted and sold in our market area covering the Pacific Northwest. I noticed that our company was concentrating on the larger paper mills and semi-conductor accounts, but no one was really calling on the smaller accounts and alternative industries such as food and beverage, trucking, wood treatment, plywood, and smaller chemical industries. To reach my personal goal I started implementing a marketing system for these new customers where I would work a different geographical area and community every day and when I completed all those areas that made up our local metropolitan region,

I would repeat it, creating a type of schedule, so my customers would become accustomed to seeing me on a regular basis. One day I would call on the northwest section of town, then the southwest, and so on. During those days I always tried to call on one completely new company and introduce myself, trying to find out what they do and who the main players were that purchase the products and services I represent. Sometimes the receptionist would introduce me to the maintenance manager, the plant manager, their purchasing agent, plant engineer or even the owner. Sometimes I would strike out and get nowhere, except possibly a name and a phone number, or information on the best way to make an appointment. Remember those receptionists are just doing their job. If I get introduced to a decision maker, it's an opportunity to present myself, trying to build rapport, and show my wares and services. During this time, you might see something in their office that is personal to them such as a photograph of a fishing trip, golf outing, mountain climbing, a diploma, or an unusual item like a piece of glassware. Making a comment on their personal items can start a conversation which can build a comfort level and rapport with the customer and can lead into a future business relationship. During this time of communication, you can discover what types of products or services that you can provide their organization, while touching on their features and benefits.

You do need to be flexible with the market area, certain areas or accounts need only be seen bi-monthly, once a quarter or possibly a couple times a year, depending on location and the demands for your services. Your intuition on when to set up appointments with new and old accounts will come into play when making these determinations. Before that customer gives you that first order for a component or service, you must do your best to give him information on confirming the pricing, that proper codes are met, confirm the terms and conditions of the agreement, along with the shipping and delivery dates, installation schedules, warrantees, any prepayment schedules, timelines of events if it is a larger project and information on any subcontractors. Information such as this is best covered prior to executing the contract. Do whatever you can to assist your customer, he is now your employer and you work for him. You are now part of your customer's team. Your integrity and reputation are on the line, just as it is every day. It has taken me sometimes two to three years or longer to develop a strong business relationship. Once this connection is made, the personal and business information you exchange with your customer can become rewarding financially and personally.

One of the biggest problems with people succeeding in sales is that they do not know when to stop talking and just listen; just listen to what your customer is saying and asking. Remember the rule, if you talk longer than three minutes to a customer, you might as well just excuse yourself and depart, because the exchange of thoughts, ideas, and the act of dialogue and discussion become extremely more difficult to salvage. People like to talk about themselves, so let your customers talk. They like being the main point of attention, especially if they are at their place of employment. They like to feel important - everyone does. If you don't give them a chance to be the main focal point, they start thinking of you as a loudmouth, arrogant, self-centered "know it all" salesperson. The potential customer may end up cutting you off and there goes your future customer.

Hopefully things will go well when you meet with your customers, and you reach a conclusion. It is at this point you can utilize a closure statement such as, "If you are pleased with all the information, all I need to proceed is a PO or a signature." and then be quiet. I would sometimes keep silent for an agonizing five minutes or more. Finally, after the brutal waiting time had passed, I would then end up with the PO or signed contract.

A very important point in selling is that once you have the signed contract or purchase order in your hand from the customer, thank him and tell him you need to get the process moving and depart. This will show a sense of urgency and concern by placing your customer's business first. Also, departing quickly will not give the customer the opportunity for additional questions that may kill the order. As an example, the customer may say, "Is the color of the device blue? We really need it to be red." or "Will the unit be delivered already assembled? If not, we will have to cancel the order and determine what the extra costs will be.".

A learning rule:

- When you ask for the order or make your closing remark, STOP TALKING!
- Once you receive the order, thank your customer and depart so you can get the project or order moving. You want no opportunity for unexpected questions or issues to arise that may sabotage all your arduous work.

Throughout my selling career most of my employers have given out sales goals. Just about every time they did this, I would put the document into the bottom drawer of my desk or file it away into some hidden place in my laptop. I think it is quite ironic that your manager who probably has never sold for a living (and if they did, they fail at it) gives out sales goals created by some corporate person with no knowledge of the market, located far away and expect their sales team to achieve those goals. A good salesperson just wants to sell as much as possible anyway, so they can keep their job, and increase their income via as many profitable sales as possible.

I had a boss that always asked me if I was going to make my sales goal for the new year in January when I had eleven months ahead of me. My response was that I would sell as much as possible. Why won't I sell as much as I could? Everybody wins! I have seen many salespeople become obsessed with their yearly goals, to the point that they have difficulty functioning and get stressed out to the point of failing. They become too concerned about closing sales instead of building good business relationships that can provide business throughout their selling career.

Goals are good, if they are your goals. My goals were always greater and more long term than any I have ever been given. That way, managers, supervisors, and corporate people who hand out sales goals will not affect my performance in the marketplace. Lesson learned here is that you accept the goals they hand you with an understanding attitude and then just go out into the marketplace and do the best possible job you can. You will have a better attitude and a more enjoyable time, even with all the ups and downs that the business world may send your way.

CHAPTER 12

The Expert From Out of Town

During my time selling, an interesting thing occurred several times. Whenever a factory representative or regional/corporate manager came to visit our office, they always wanted to go on sales calls. I thought of this as the "Expert from Out of Town or EOT". This was a required task item on their annual review to receive a merit increase in their pay. Normally my strategy was to make as many appointments as possible. This would show how hard I work and demonstrate how serious I was about my job. I always tried to close orders on these appointments and show my ability at closing profitable sales. At the end of the day the visiting out-of-towner had a different view of what it takes to keep existing business and develop new customers. On occasions these out-of-towners were a little arrogant and start acting like they are in command and have all the business power and knowledge. I just let them do and say what they will because I am the one who has the relationship with the customer. After the EOT departs, sometimes I would need to contact my customer and do damage control by setting the facts straight about what the EOT had stated. I try to be honest with my customers and keep them informed that I am the one who must follow through on any promises the EOT has made. Mostly though, I try to use those EOTs to my benefit by exploiting their knowledge of our products or services.

These EOTs do show the customer that you are part of a larger team with accessible technical knowledge. Also, if there is a question of warrantee or contract execution, upper management or manufacture representatives can help resolve disputes, define terminology and resolve questions concerning agreement terms and conditions.

Once I had to bring in a regional HVAC digital controls specialist who had management and pricing responsibilities for large control projects. I was quoting a large HVAC Direct Digital Controls project with a very good customer of mine whom I had been doing business with for several years. The controls project was so large that the customer needed competitive pricing. I had enough experience to know that the project should sell for about $250-350K. I could not believe it when the regional person sent me a quote for $415K.

As soon as I saw the selling price, I knew we were not going to be awarded the project. I was left trying to explain our outrageous pricing. We were not the winners on this one. Our competition took the project for $265K. The only thing I can think of was the manager who issued the sell price did not want the project. Maybe he was too busy with other projects or maybe he just did not price the project correctly. For whatever reason, his pricing was not realistic and made me and our local office appear like we were out of touch with the local market. To tell you the truth I conveyed this to the customer. It wasn't like we didn't have a good reputation or a high-quality product. The EOT pricing manager, I believe, just did not want the job or maybe he had other projects booked and had already utilized all his resources and felt we could not deliver in a timely and professional matter. For me, either way I lost the sale and some confidence in my abilities with my customer.

The lesson here is: I should convince upper management to allow me to price the project without using the regional manager. Sometimes staying local is the best way to do business. Be mindful of the EOT, use them to your advantage to develop your business.

CHAPTER 13

Control Your Emotions

An emotional decision can be dangerous. There was a recent article about decision making and how decisions are best made after a good night's sleep. I have experienced that staying calm during discussions is a good thing. Emotions such as humor or empathy can be worthy, but anger can destroy relationships. You may win an argument, but at the same time lose a relationship. When you control your emotions, you will be a person who has command over negative occurrences that can be corrected and who can try and improve the situation.

I had a manager once who I found out later did not want to hire me as his salesperson to grow the company's service business. He just wanted to keep the operation small, so he could manage it without any additional stressful responsibilities. Unfortunately for him, and fortunately for me, his company's management directed him to hire me as their salesperson because they were trying to grow their business and he didn't want the added responsibilities or extra work. I was their first factory service salesperson. They presented me with a decent salary and an incentive package. All I needed to do was hit a certain profit number and then anything beyond that would pay out as extra income. That also meant I needed to cover all my costs that were applied such as salary, sales expenses like taking customers out to lunch, company car, sales training and medical insurance. Covering your total cost will put in a stronger position with the company.

One day I brought in a project that was to upgrade the HVAC controls for a few bank facilities for a national financial banking company that needed to be discussed with my manager. A few weeks had passed and we still had not met to go over the details of the project. One morning I mentioned that we needed to discuss the HVAC controls project and I had some free time to do so. He said that we could meet that morning. I had an appointment later that morning and other customers to see. I was getting my sales folders and literature together, placing them on a chair by the front door next to his office, preparing to depart. My manager came storming out of his office yelling at me about not giving him enough time for us to meet concerning the project. I followed him into his office and sat down while he was still yelling at me the whole time. I remained as calm as I could, not saying a word. He was still yelling about being rushed and not meeting when we should have. Remaining calm, I said in a very pleasant low-keyed voice: "we can discuss the project right now". After a few moments of him ranting and raving on, he noticed that I was just sitting there listening to him yelling away. A calmness came over his facial expression and then he quieted down and relaxed. We then had our discussion concerning my new project which took about five minutes. He gave me the information I needed so I could contact the customer and move the selling process along, closing the sale.

During that episode I sensed that my manager realized he was out of control and suddenly became embarrassed in front of his new young salesman.

Lesson learned: the calm, level-headed person who has command over their emotions is the one who usually has the clearer mind and more control of disagreements and problematic situations.

I always strive to control my emotions and be as ethical as possible in my business dealings. This is how you build integrity in the market-place. When you lose control of your emotions you can lose customers, and customers prefer to do business with people who are in command and remedy problems when things start going in the wrong direction.

CHAPTER 14

Sometimes You Need to Walk Away

In business negotiations when the competition has the inside track, or the customer is asking for items that are not realistic; you may just thank the customer for the business opportunity and just walk away rather than ending up living with a nonprofitable headache. Remember, your time is valuable. You do not want to waste your time on something that has no chance of succeeding. Use your intuitive and analytical judgement whether to proceed.

There was a national insurance facility that occupied one of the largest office buildings in our city and was managed by an east coast commercial property management company. The building was around thirty floors and had a large physical plant on the roof where two large mechanical air conditioning machines serviced the building. One of the air conditioning machines had a major compressor failure and out competitor was trying to sell the customer on a new replacement machine. Fortunately, I had a good relationship with the building manager, and he contacted me requesting a proposal on repairing the unit. Our repair cost was $119K while the competitor's replacement cost was $220K. We received the purchase order for the repair, saving the customer a substantial amount of money. The building engineer was upset because he wanted our competitor to sell them a new air conditioning unit, but the manager overruled him.

About five months later the building engineer contacted me about one of their other buildings that had a large air conditioning compressor that had failed and wanted me to present a proposal on replacing the failed compressor. I knew he would be receiving a proposal from my competitor for the same repair. Our in-house staff would need to obtain pricing on the Original Equipment Manufacture (OEM) compressor and parts.

We also needed pricing on a crane company to remove the failed compressor and place the new compressor on the roof, and we needed pricing for the electrical work. I took all this pricing information and put my proposal together. I wanted this project, so we priced the job very competitively. Then I delivered the proposal to the customer.

Like a good salesperson, I asked when they would be making their buying decision. I contacted the customer the following week. The building engineer informed me that my price was indeed the lowest. I had beaten my competitor and was excited to receive the order for the project. Our sell price for the project was $33K. The customer then stated he needed to contact my competitor and let them reprice their proposal. Of course I asked him why he would do such a thing, and he said he felt obligated to give them a second chance because he had done so much business with them in the past. I let him know that both our companies use the same union with trained journeymen level technicians. It did not matter to him; he gave the project to the competitor anyway.

For me, this was an ethical conflict of interest because the building engineer could not be trusted to review proposals fairly and honestly. I felt I would be wasting my time to respond to any future requests for proposals from this person. The facility manager was an old friend of mine whom I had performed numerous projects for over the years. A few weeks later I had breakfast with him and told him I would do business with anyone in their organization except their building engineer who gave my competitor my pricing along with a second chance to reprice their proposal. I kept in touch with this company, calling on other personnel, but I would not do any more dealings with the building engineer.

When creating a proposal there are people and time involved which cost you and your company money, and if you are not awarded the project that cost hits your bottom line as a loss. The cost for our company to create that proposal was approximately $1,500 which is normal for a project of this size. Some proposals can be created quickly at low cost while other long-term and complicated projects and agreements can cost into the range of hundreds of thousands of dollars. It is one thing for a buyer to shop a proposal price without the salesperson's knowledge, but to tell a salesperson that their price is low and that they are going to give your competitor your pricing so they can reprice their own proposal is just unethical.

Don't beat a dead horse and don't waste your time on people who will not operate in an ethical and professional manner.

CHAPTER 15

Make Your Customer Comfortable

Over the years I have met many good people who have helped me succeed in closing profitable business and build strong relationships. One thing I have learned from them is when meeting with your customers, try to make them feel comfortable. This will help you succeed in creating strong business relationships and increase your sales.

I noticed when I first appear before a customer that I will mirror some of their personality traits. How are they sitting? Are they leaning forward in a communicated and focused position, or are they sitting back in their chair, relaxed and calm in a thoughtful position? I catch myself sitting sometimes using the same posture they are using. As my customer speaks, is it in a relaxing but confident cadence? I find myself following their personality. Does the person get right to the point and ask you where you are from and what you are selling, or does the buyer wish to just talk about minor items of conversation such as the weather, some sporting event, or the mounted trophy he has hanging from his office wall prior to discussing any business? This type of introductory conversation is an icebreaker and is very important as a foundation builder of personal common ground that develops rapport.

You need to get a feeling for the time the customer has a available to spend with you. I always try to be sure to thank the person for taking time from their busy day to spend with me. If the person is rushed, tell him you will be as quick as possible covering the items that need to be addressed. This type of customer will appreciate you understanding how critical their time is. Possibly during your next visit, they will have more time to spend with you. For example, there was a large local brewery that took me two years to develop a good business relationship with. I was able to arrive without an appointment and wait for my customer to have a few free minutes to speak with me. I would ask if I could survey his inventory for any items that needed replenishing. One day I showed up early in the afternoon and he told me that they were brewing a new beer from the Midwest for the owner of the brewery and asked me if I wanted to try some. That afternoon, myself and three of my customers from the brewery ended up in the basement drinking the new brew the rest of the day. It's this kind of occurrence in selling that makes all the disappointments tolerable. From that day on my relationship became very strong with that customer and my business with them increased.

Being relaxed and calm in front of a customer is very important. This is difficult to do when things start falling apart, like when your delivery was four months later than what you originally told your customer, or the components you sold did not operate the way they were supposed to operate. Honesty and calmness are the best way to approach these situations. It always seems the person who remains calm and has their emotions under control mostly prevails when things start going sideways. They seem to have some presence of control over a troubled occurrence.

Also, be creative in solving problems. What can we do differently? What options do we have? Can the factory look at their distribution network to see if they might locate the needed component? If the component does not operate correctly, will the warranty or a retrofit solve the problem quickly? Solving the customer's problems quickly can decrease their down time in production, saving them a loss in manufacturing and helping to supply their customers more quickly. By assisting your customer in solving problems you will become a part of their team. When they start calling you with their problems and you can offer them solutions, you will start feeling like a hero and the relationship will grow stronger.

It is all the small things that add up to building business relationships. Sometimes it happens quickly in a day or a few weeks, other times it may take months or even years.

There are times when I think sales has an element of hypnosis. Follow their mood, stay relaxed and calm. Try to use their name when addressing your customer. A person likes to hear their own name during conversations - it shows respect.

Make sure your appearance is presentable and you are dressed for the weather. Wear a sports coat, raincoat, or an overcoat. If you wear a hat, take it off when you enter their place of business. Be polite and courteous. Try to give a smile that is warm and honest. People usually do not like frowns! Don't act out, be sincere and genuine. Remember your customer has seen numerous salespeople over the years and can spot someone putting on a front. They can see right through someone who is acting out. Most good salespeople use their own personalities to connect with their customer. You will have a challenging time in making appointments with decision makers if you do not come across as a real genuine person versus someone who is putting on a false appearance just to make a sale.

It is a funny and amazing world we live in. You never know who you may encounter or who you may end up speaking with or talking to on the phone. The receptionist you first meet one day may be the purchasing agent you are trying to sell to a few months later. The person push-ing the broom could end up the maintenance manager or the facilities director. This advancement of people to a level of decision makers has happened numerous times over my career. Do not treat anyone with disrespect because you never know... someday they may be in a position of authority making buying decisions!

One day during an appointment with one of my best customers, I watched a fellow salesperson start speaking with a Texas accent just like the customer. I asked him about the sudden transformation in his ac-cent and he said he once lived in Texas, and it comes back when he is around other people with that accent. A couple of weeks later I landed a $150K order from that customer.

Remember, mirroring a person's actions unconsciously can produce a relaxed and comfortable atmosphere for conducting and building strong business relationships.

CHAPTER 16

Save Money for the Unexpected

You never know what the future may hold, so being prepared economically for the unexpected is probably the best way to handle those unpleasant situations. One day everything is roses and the next might be poison ivy!

My father, being a purchasing agent, saw many salespeople come and go. He told me once to always be prepared for the unexpected and save your money because you never know what the future holds. You could lose your position or even your employment at the drop of a hat. And that is exactly what happened to me.

After twenty-four years of making large profits for the company I was selling for, one morning I was given a cardboard box to collect my personal belongings and I was driven home by a fellow employee. This happened in July 2010 during a recession. The day I was shown the door we had seventeen employees. Today that office has only four employees. This is an example of poor corporate management, unable to see the repercussions of their decisions. They thought all those long-term service contract customers would stay even after my termination.

Upper management thought they could replace a long-term salesperson with a younger, unexperienced person and save on salary and pension payments while still retaining all the existing business. They were wrong thinking the customers would stay after terminating their long-time salesperson. Upper management may see quick increased profits for a brief time, but in the long term they lost big time!

Always try to be prepared economically for the unexpected because you never know what tomorrow may bring. You need to create your own financial security.

CHAPTER 17

Build Relationships and Know Your Cost

In sales you need to know what the true cost of your products or services are. When you know what your cost is, then you can apply your markup to obtain the profit you want to capture when the sale closes. Once you start receiving a steady flow of business from your customers, they will become comfortable with your pricing. This is one way how trust and loyalty is created, and long-term profitable business relationships are built.

My father was employed by the Alcoa Corporation for thirty-eight years. I thought this was quite an accomplishment. Looking back now, he must have been proud of his long-term career. He had a great reputation as a money maker, creating large profits and realizing when a situation was not profitable. His employer sent him across the country and even to Africa using him as their "trouble shooter", looking over the operational expenses and analyzing profit and loss numbers to determine how economically sound the business entity was. I felt I had the same abilities, going back to my young days picking strawberries and being capable of calculating exactly what my earnings were, down to the very last box of strawberries.

One of the sayings I used during my selling years was: "You need to be an asset, not a liability.". Are you making money for the company and yourself? If you are, then your stability as an employee is more secure than if you are losing money on your sales. To determine if you are profitable you need to know how much you cost the company. A quick way to find out your cost is to simply ask the company accountant or better yet look at your paycheck, your expenses, and your benefits. Once you know what you cost the company, then you know your break-even point you need to hit with your sales. This will help you justify your existence as an employee. The more profitable sales you bring in beyond your break-even point, the more chances of increasing your stability, commissions and income.

One of the dangers that faces all employees who are employed by large Fortune 500 companies is the political environments of the organizations. These huge organizations change their management structures on a regular basis. These changes of management seek to improve and grow business profitably which Wall Street is always looking for. From my experience, the long-term thinkers are best because they are looking out into the future five, ten or even twenty years trying to determine what changes may occur in the market and how best to adapt to those changes to produce a stronger profitable organization. A strong progressive research and development program that produces new products that are introduced to the market in a strategic manner can make the manufacture a leader in that industry. Research and Development has brought us the Tesla electric car, the internet, iPhone, and digital controls associated with companies like Microsoft, Intel, Amazon and Apple. As an example of working with a progressive company, I was fortunate to be part of the first sales force to be equipped with a laptop computer along with portable printers. Management referred to the laptop as a "productivity tool".

Using the laptop, the company wanted to decrease the amount of time it took to close a sale and increase the number of sales made. They were successful - my sales quantity increased! Today we have iPhones, emails, texts, and the ability to scan documents and proposals to our customers, processing business quickly.

Information can be accessed through social media and web pages. You can google a world of information. But I believe sooner or later you will need to look that customer in the eye. Both parties, buyer and seller need to know who they are dealing with on a personal basis looking each other in the eye, discovering the qualities of their character and determining trust. I swear it looks like I will be going to my grave believing that good business is based on personal relationships and not communications of emails. Technology though may change a lot of this soon with Skype or Zoom meetings to process business dealings. In the future you might be dealing with a virtually created image. Think on this while you're Skyping - are there people in the background listening in on your conversations, gathering data that you are unaware of? This may seem a little paranoid, but it is something to think about!

What about all those businesspeople utilizing all forms of transportation just to be able to meet with their customers in person. You will learn more about your customers by meeting them in person rather than through emails. In person they may be more at ease and enlighten you to the status of their company, convey personal information and interesting facts about their industry such as how they operate in the marketplace, what they expect from their vendors, who is in line for a promotion or termination, what is the future of their customers and what their customers expect. This is valuable information for dealing with your customers.

Knowing your cost, you can control your profit margins, and if you reach a point with your customer when you become a part of their team, you will secure a longer, stronger business relationship than your competitor.

CHAPTER 18

Take Advantage of Retirement Programs

Many companies have some type of retirement saving programs. This is their way of providing their employees a way to plan for well-funded retirement. Whatever the retirement program might be, 401K, profit sharing, pension, ownership in the company, shares of stock or stock options - my advice is to take advantage of it because at retirement time it will make a big difference in your financial security.

As I look back on almost forty years of selling, I spent thirty-one of those years with two of the largest Fortune 500 companies. Twenty-four of those years were spent with Carrier Corporation, an international heating, ventilation and air conditioning (HVAC) manufacturing company (a division of United Technologies), and seven years with Lockheed Martin Corporation in their energy division. I was a person who took ownership in all my business dealings. When a customer gave me an order, I did my absolute best to deliver what that customer expected. I felt my reputation was on the line and I wanted to be a salesperson who cares about the integrity of his actions in the business community and with my fellow employees. The fact remains that I was also representing my employer and selling my company along with myself. I might believe all the accounts I developed were personally mine, but they were the company's accounts. That was my job - build the business, increase the account base, make money for the company. Companies can change territories and/or the products you sell. If they wish they can take away all your arduous work developing a new customer base. One day you might be selling in the southern territory and the next day you must start all over in a new northern territory. One day selling Product A and the next you can only sell Product B. Managers can set you up to fail by giving you goals that are completely unattainable. Be aware and cognizant of situations such as this as this might be a political movement to eliminate you.

If the corporation has any kind of retirement program, take full advantage of it - the sooner the better. At one time pensions were common but now it seems we only have 401K savings programs. What happened to pensions? I believe the upper managers (CFOs, CEOs, etc.) are driven by the constant demands of the shareholders of Wall Street want that money to increase profits, therefore increasing the demand for company shares and creating higher salaries for higher management executives in the company. Pensions may have also been the victim of rising health insurance costs.

Today we mainly have the 401K programs. If your company has a 401K or any other type of profit-sharing saving program, use it the best you can. Whenever possible, max out your 401K because the day will arrive when retirement is upon you and whatever preparations you have made will be your future financial security (unless you have some type of family inheritance, or your spouse is the bucket of gold at the end of your career rainbow). Either way, it's better to be prepared than wishing you had taken advantage of a retirement savings program.

I once knew an employee who had been employed with a company for over eighteen years and never took advantage of their 401K program - it probably cost him at least $500K before taxes. As you get closer to your retirement, try to increase your contributions to your 401K as high as you can prior to taxes. I increased my contributions from 10 to 23% as I got closer to retirement. The larger amount you have in a 401K the faster it grows, and you can pay the taxes as you withdraw the amount during retirement. If your retirement account is making a 6% growth, take 4% and you can grow the account at 2% and have a self-funding retirement fund that never depletes. Also, you should have a professional financial advisor assisting you in managing your retirement wealth.

The more prepared you are financially for retirement, the more financially comfortable you will be during your retirement.

CHAPTER 19

There is Always Change

One constant in our lives is that change is always present as we confront those changes, those peaks and valleys, we need to find the strength to create stability as we persevere into our future.

In the Fortune 500 corporations, you will sooner or later encounter their Human Resources (HR) department. Early in my corporate selling career I was naive and believed HR was there to protect you from being treated unfairly by managers who may try to undermine your efforts. I know it sounds strange that a manager would want to terminate a profitable salesperson, but emotions and egos can interfere with logical thinking. If it is not broken, why fix it? With all the personalities, egos and emotional interactions, poor decisions can be made. Sometimes managers will set you up to fail so they can promote their own agenda making you the "fall guy". You don't want to be the one viewing the world from under the bus as it runs you over. Speak your mind diplomatically and honestly about situations that are unfair. Have someone in your company that you trust and can discuss your situations with, and strategize to avoid unpleasant occurrences. When things go south you will need someone on your side. A sounding board to confirm that your actions will help and not harm.

My main strategy was to sell as much as possible. This way management should leave you alone because they are too busy managing all those projects and orders you sold. They should be purchasing components, scheduling services, progressing billings, and organizing labor instead of harassing you. You should want to create the largest possible backlog of projects and orders as possible so your company will be too occupied dealing with all the new business you have brought in. That way you can focus on building more sales. I had the immense pleasure to associate with some of the best salespeople around and several times I thought about the manager who would be thinking: "Oh my God, you did what I asked you to do! You sold it, now what am I going to do?". Many times I felt that I was in this situation where management could not keep up with the business I was bringing through the door. Because of this, I am sure that company is why I was never offered a management position, even when I requested it of them. Early on I always wanted to create my own sales team and give them the independence, support, and energy to perform. HR seems to be completely out of touch with salespeople who perform, not understanding the corporate roadblocks faced every day by good salespeople. HR seems to be mainly concerned with the possibility of internal lawsuits against the company. Other times HR seems to be nothing more than a puppet of upper management. So, keep your eyes and ears open and be safe. As it was once said to me: "Sometimes it is best to keep your head below the radar.".

Usually at the beginning of a calendar year the sales force is given their incentive/commission program. One salesperson within the first six months went out into his market and maximized the incentive program. The company was to pay him a six-figure dollar amount for his efforts. The company then hired a new president who changed the incentive/commission program reducing the amount the salesperson was to receive by more than 35% of the original incentive amount. The salesperson resigned, got a lawyer and sued the company on breach of contract for not following through on the original incentive agreement.

Luckily the salesperson kept all his emails which stated that he would be rewarded on the higher program from the previous year. The lawsuit lasted about two years, costing both sides a tremendous amount of time and legal fees. The salesperson won the case and settled for around 1.5 million dollars. Just because some new corporate president wanted to show the board of directors that he could increase profits immediately, it ended up costing the company massive amounts of money. HR should have given the original incentive payment in the beginning and the company would not have lost all that money. So, be aware and get good legal counselling before taking on the corporate machine - it can be danger to your mental and physical health, not to mention your finances.

Customers are like us, they do not like surprises. You keep changing salespeople, managers or service personnel and your company will lose respect in the marketplace. Customers like consistency. Why do you go to the same grocery store, dentist, coffee shop or clothing store? Because you have a relationship with them. There are no surprises. You are treated with a friendly smile and knowledgeable service people. HR needs to be aware and learn from situations such as these. Unfortunately, HR usually gets involved too late. They should be reviewing the backgrounds of managers prior to hiring. I was once notified one day that I should return to the office to meet my new manager. He lasted only five months and was terminated due to failure to deliver on terms of a service contract with a major customer. After his departure, I discovered that he was in the process of suing his previous employer. Why would anyone hire someone who is suing their last employer? I was amazed. Background checks should always be conducted prior to hiring a person or you may end up in court or lose a lot of your good customers.

How we deal with difficult or pleasant changes will determine whether the outcomes become acceptable. State focused on your mission, selling and let the changes around you roll away like water on a duck's back. Do your best to accept changes when they occur. Almost always remember, when one door closes a new one will open.

CHAPTER 20

Stay Close to Your Customer

I have always felt that if you take care of those who take care of you that your future will be much more enjoyable and possibly quite profitable. Staying close to your customers will help build stronger and longer relationships.

It was November 2, 1986, the first day of employment with Carrier Corporation, an international company providing HVAC equipment. The parent company, United Technologies, was so large at the time that they employed globally well over two hundred thousand people. The office I was employed with was one of their many factory aftermarket service branches for commercial applications such as hospital, commercial office buildings, industrial facilities, and educational facilities. We were responsible for equipment startups, warranties, energy and control upgrades, and maintenance programs. My previous employment was selling for a company representing industrial instrumentation and Carrier had been one of my many customers.

There were benefits working for a large international company that I was not used to such as a new company vehicle every two years, annual cost of living increases, and factory training in HVAC equipment and sales. About once every four months or so I would travel to a large city like Los Angeles, Phoenix or San Francisco and on a few occasions to the east coast for training and meetings. All these remote gatherings were great for developing company loyalty, pride and a sense that you are part of a much larger team that would support you and your customers.

I worked out of one of their Pacific Northwest offices, serving the northwest market. When you looked at our western region, our market area was producing a large profit. All large corporations and good companies wish to have steady growth with good profit margins. At my previous employer I was paid straight commission, so I was driven by profit. I was still young with a mortgage, along with my wife and our three young children. My new employer presented me with their incentive program for selling that was based on the amount of profit you could generate. Of course I wanted to maximize my income by capturing as much profitable business as possible.

Fear of failure sometimes can be a good motivator. When I first started selling for my new employer my manager gave me a list of all their commercial equipment with location information within our territory of southwest Washington and the state of Oregon. I thought this was excellent information. I started out selling with the concept that every one of our machines should have a preventive maintenance program. So one by one, I went through that list and systematically contacted, in person, every customer on that list.

After more than nine months our service business started increasing at a fast rate. We needed to start hiring more technicians and office staff to handle the increase in business and I started making more money. The problem was that the branch manager was not used to the increased business and all the service calls by our new customers. He once was a service technician, a union man, who was asked to manage this small service branch. We had about eight service technicians, two office staff, a service manager, and an HVAC controls engineer when I was hired. I discovered later that the branch manager did not want to hire a salesperson and was forced to do so by upper management. One morning the branch service manager pulled me aside and told me what an excellent job I was doing bringing in all the new service business and that the branch was doing very well. The next thing he said really surprised me as he asked me to just stay in the office and answer service calls on the phone. I was quite shocked since I made my income by increasing the business of the branch which generated incentive/commission payments based on the number of profits my sales created. I smiled at my manager and said "no problem" and then I just kept selling as much as I could. That manager did not like the growth in business because, I believe, he did not want the extra responsibility and work that was involved. He also knew that the company would want him to continue that rate of growth and they would increase the branch's performance goals.

Having come from a straight commission-based job, it was simple to calculate my income. It was based on the number of profits generated from sales. But what I soon discovered is that a large corporation sometimes will change their incentive/commission programs annually. As soon as you understand how one incentive program works, a new year starts with a completely new program that you must learn and adapt to. After several years working for a company like this, a pattern began to emerge. upper management would change about every three to five years. The new president would want to generate higher profits for the board of directors and Wall Street causing the stock values to increase. A quick and uncomplicated way to do this was to decrease the incentive/commission payment programs for the sales force. For example, one year I was making a good six figure income. The following year I sold approximately the same growth amount, bringing in good profits for the company, but my income dropped by 35%. The new company president increased the company's profits tremendously and surely captured a large bonus. At the same time, almost all the salespeople left the company for new employment that offered much better incentive/commission programs. Those departing salespeople took most of their customers with them. But, during the interviewing process that new president convinced the company managers that he could increase the company's profits with a new incentive/commission program along with reorganizing personnel, streamlining production and re-assigning key support positions. Phrases such as "do more with less" and "value engineering" start appearing in company conversations, and if you try to do more with less you will set yourself up to fail.

This president who made all these short term quick profit producing changes left the company at the end of about four years and was hired by one of our competitors and received a signing bonus of over one million dollars. I stayed with the company mainly because I was grandfathered into their pension plan and my 401K was growing at a strong rate. I had also developed a large customer base which continued to grow, and due to my seniority secured over five weeks of paid vacation along with twelve holidays. I believed I had created some financial security for my family.

Customers expect good deliveries and reliable equipment and if they do not receive what they are accustomed to, they move their business somewhere else. Innovative technologies and creative procedures do make a difference and can increase the customer retention and satisfactions.

When you are out in the marketplace representing yourself and your company, you don't want to be explaining to your customers about all the reorganizations and personnel changes going on within your company. The customer will end up seeing a decline in service and product quality and they will start looking elsewhere for a better vendor. Customers talk with one another at industrial trade shows and social gatherings. Many times I have heard from my own customers, "I am never going to do business with that company ever again!". Someone did not follow through on an agreement. A deadline was not made. There were too many extra costs added to a project. The vendor did not honor an agreed price, or their service technician did shoddy work possibly causing a down time in production or a discomfort to that customer.

What happens to a corporation that gets too huge? Sometimes they lose touch with their customers. For without customers, you have no business. Unemployment does not sound very appealing. The old saying, "the only thing that never changes is that there is always change" comes to mind. Every day is different, people come and people go and it is how we adapt to change that makes us strong. One day you have a great relationship with a person in upper management who lets you know what direction the company is moving, or a new person is going to be placed in a new position, and the next day they leave for a new position with another company. It is good to have a friend outside your company that you can discuss difficult relationships you may have with your employer and fellow workers. To make good decisions, it is best to get different opinions and views of situations. Looking at the pros and cons of a decision prior to making a final determination is a good way to proceed.

Dealing with the internal operations of large corporations can be more difficult than closing a sale. I have a good friend who sells large contracts for goods and services and recently captured a $50 million agreement. His company, however, had the agreement stalled in their legal and contracts department as they reviewed the terms and conditions. The customer wanted very much to move ahead on the agreement but walked away because they were under a time schedule and were getting frustrated that the company was taking too long to approve the terms and conditions of the agreement. Lesson learned: I would have tried to communicate up front with the contracts and legal team about how critical the timeline of events for the approval process was and I would prepare the customer about the timing of those events.

Why do you go to a certain gas station, pharmacy, grocery store or restaurant? Possibly you feel comfortable there, you have a pleasant rapport with the staff, the location is convenient, the environment is clean and inviting and there is a sense of consistency. There are no surprises. Your expectations are met. This is what upper corporate management misses when they get too involved analyzing accounting spread sheets showing trends of costs and profit and loss figures. They lose touch with where those numbers come from. Those sales accounting figures represent relationships between people doing business. If you increase a sales price without a good explanation, you could lose your customer. If you don't respond to your customer's needs, they will find someone else who will. Another saying comes to mind, "take care of those who take care of you, and things will work out.". When things go south with a customer and they contact you because you had helped them out in the past, they are giving you an opportunity to resolve their problem. It is not good when your customer has a problem and they don't call you for help.

Stay close to your customers as much as possible. You can learn valuable information that can assist you in future dealings, and when problems arise hopefully they will call you instead of your competition.

CHAPTER 21

Do the Best You Can

During your business day, always try to care for your customers the best you possibly can. Sometimes you will succeed and other times you may fail, but knowing that you have done your best will strengthen your confidence and toughen your resilience.

During my employment with Carrier, I experienced branch managers being promoted to regional positions as part of the new management team and then when that management group ran its course, those promoted would be demoted back to the branch manager or to their original positions. I saw one individual go up and down the promotional ladder four times. Basically, the promoted branch manager failed at that regional position each time and then he would be returned to his previous branch manager position. Likely this was due to the idea that the new regional manager could not hire new personnel because he was given no funding to do so. I was baffled and amazed that they would promote a person into a higher salary position that he had failed at previously four times.

I survived this corporate shuffle of ups and downs by just staying focused on my assigned position by bringing in the sales and just taking care of the customer, and at the same time keeping my customers isolated from the corporate changes. Pretty simple you would think. It worked well until the company started thinking they could increase profits by replacing me with a younger, cheaper model. They looked at my salary, 401K balance and pension and thought, hey we can save the company $35-45K per year in costs and increase our profits by replacing him with a younger new hire.

One morning our regional manager was in town and wanted to meet with me and the branch service manager. The regional manager walked into the conference room, closed the door behind him and started yelling at me saying, "how old are you?". Needless to say I was surprised. He proceeded to blame me for the state of the economy (it was February 2010 and the recession was going strong). Unemployment was at a high for Oregon at 7.5%. After being yelled at my branch manager quickly exited the conference room. This was the same regional manager who had been up and down the promotional corporate ladder four times. He knew me from the last time he was in this regional position, and I had a feeling then that his last demotion was somehow connected to me and he was out for payback. I was just a salesperson trying to keep the branch business profitable and steady during an economic recession. Our business was strong with no decreases and we were keeping a constant flow of business coming through the door. If this regional manager had come to me with a reasonable severance package, I would have probably accepted it.

That was February 2010. At the meeting I thought this regional manager wanted me to get up from my chair and knuckle him in the nose (not that he didn't deserve it!). I felt like doing it, but I knew better. I was not going to fall for that kind of action. I believe this is what he truly wanted me to do, but I am more professional than that. Instead, I sat there red-faced mad and did nothing - only listened. I knew if I did punch him I would be fired on the spot and out the door with HR and legal corporate people following me. With all that happened, I knew my career with this company would be coming to a quick end. I felt I only had about six months at the most. I had almost twenty-four years of my life with this company building a strong business. I had a responsibility to my family as a provider, so I sat there and bit my lip. If I had punched him it would have ended right then and there. I believe he was taunting me and wanted me to hit him. I was more mature than that. Controlling my emotions and doing my best to remain calm paid off.

After that terrible and insulting meeting, I met with a couple of my fellow employees after work at a local sports bar. I told them that I would be gone before the end of the year. They didn't believe me, but I had seen occurrences like this happen in the past within the company and knew what type of person this regional manager was. His reputation was not the best - arrogant and self-centered. I heard that he was disliked by others in the company as well. In the corporate world, top management can be the type of people who can talk the talk, financially or just have the political savvy with a strong ego and intellectual smarts to sustain their positions. This statement may sound strong, but it often occurs more than we like, and this regional manager fit the description. There are environments where good leaders and managers do exist, all you need to do is listen to the news and read the business articles. There are so many creative and successful companies: Nike, Microsoft, Apple, Tesla, Lockheed Martin, Boeing - with leaders who have vision and treat their employees fairly. As a salesperson you visit all types of successful companies. As you enter their lobbies and are greeted by their receptionist you sometimes can feel the organization has a happy and productive atmosphere, and other times it can have a stressed and unpleasant feeling. Remember, if you take care of the people who take care of you, usually good things happen.

The company I had spent the last twenty-four years with started feeling as if it was becoming disconnected due to its size (sixty billion in revenues). So, what was a little service branch in Oregon worth? Not much. But, if you multiply it by a hundred, the number of service branches across the country combined revenues were somewhat impressive! What happened is that the corporate office lost touch with the customer. The financial reports become the only thing they could relate to, and they did not realize that those numbers were actual people who put trust in us as a company to deliver what they requested and expected. The corporation lost touch with the understanding that each business transaction was a relationship between a salesperson and their customer. When numbers become the center of action for a corporation without the understanding of the relationships behind those financial reports, their world of business starts to diminish.

Don't get me wrong, accountants with their profit and loss financial reports are a very critical part of understanding where you are and how you plan to proceed with your business. Financial information is valuable, and it assists in making good business decisions. But it should also include the local manager along with his sales team on how best to move the business forward using the knowledge of their local market they service.

The lesson here is that one can only do the best they can to adjust to the every-changing world of the corporate ebb and flow of management changes. A good friend of mine once told me, "Keep your head below the radar". Concentrate on doing your job the best you can and don't get caught up in the whirl of upper corporate politics. Your numbers will reveal your efforts and will hopefully give you a feeling of security.

At the end of the day, knowing you did everything you could to satisfy your customer and those you associate with is all you can really do, and move on to your next challenge.

CHAPTER 22

Stay Ahead of Your Competition

In the business world one needs to be aware of what the competition is doing in order to respond to your market. Companies are always trying to present new products and their services to their customers to differentiate themselves to become the leaders in their market and industry. Staying in tune with the newest trends will help you remain in the forefront in your market. During my career, if I had the opportunity, I would ask my customers what my competitors were doing so I could respond accordingly.

During my early years with Carrier, I was fortunate that they invested substantial amounts of their profits towards research and development. They explored the innovative technologies and applied those new developments to the marketplace. At the time the company was the world's largest manufacturer of HVAC equipment, and I was part of their outside sales force for their aftermarket services in southwest Washington and the state of Oregon. This research and development kept Carrier in the forefront of their industry throughout the world.

One of the technical advancements the company applied to their national service sales force team was a new portable computer. At the time operations were well into utilizing the computer for billing, inventory control and communications, but it had never been introduced to the sales force. They divided the country into two halves for training and introduced their latest sales tool: the laptop computer. I was part of the western division and about fifty of us were flown to St. Louis for a week of training on the new laptop. They referred to the laptop as a "productivity tool". It was a wonderful time saver!

The training showed us how to use Microsoft Word, Excel, how to file and organize all your customer contact information. They also provided us with a portable printer so you could create and edit proposal and legal documents in the field. No longer would you need to return to the office to create or correct proposals. You could even have your customer assist you and the wording of your proposals to fit their requirements. Instead of working on proposals at your office, you could now work on them at home, at a hotel while traveling, even a café or coffee shop. With the new portable laptop, a tremendous amount of time could be saved, and proposals can be tailored to your customer's liking and delivered quickly.

Today we have iPhones and laptops. Documents can be scanned or emailed remotely to the customer. Everything seems to be instantaneous. But sometimes you may feel it necessary to obtain a signature on a contract or an original purchase order for a proposal in person. Questions may arise concerning terms and conditions, or delivery specifications that can be addressed quickly and personally on the spot. Other times multi-million dollar projects can take up to a year or even much longer to close which will take patience.

If a customer gives you only a verbal acceptance to your proposal, then you need to get the contract or purchase order signed to have a binding agreement. This is when the agreement becomes legal and binding. All the emails, texts, Faxes, or conversations mean nothing until you have that signed document.

Throughout my career there have been many times I heard salespeople state that they have the order and when I ask them if they have a signature or a purchase order and they said no, then I tell them they really don't have anything. A sale is closed only when the paperwork is complete with a signed contract or purchase order from the customer showing acceptance by both parties, through the offer, the RFP or proposal, and the acceptance with a signed contract or the issue of a purchase order.

At the end of the day you need to feel that you have that special something, that extra edge that your competition doesn't have. That added knowledge of products, scheduling, and pricing that your competition doesn't have can put you in the winner's circle, especially when you have in your possession as a signed contract or purchase order.

CHAPTER 23

Be Prepared for Cultural Changes

We live in a changing world and how we adapt to those changes will help us relate to our volatile and fluctuating market. Keep your eyes and ears open to those changes and you will become more capable of securing more comfortable and stronger business relationships.

Everyone has some type of morning routine. We are awakened by a clock radio or possibly just wake at a specific time because we have been going to work at that time for so long. Your morning routines probably include showering, brushing teeth, normal grooming for the day's business activities. As a salesperson, you should have an assortment of at least five pairs of shoes from casual to formal business. Men should have several dress shirts and a few formal suites, and for the women the same holds true with dresses or pant suits.

Make sure your shoes are shined and clean, your slacks and shirts pressed. I recommend developing a relationship with a good dry cleaner, and on a regular schedule have your work shirts cleaned, starched and pressed. For different weather you should have a raincoat and even an overcoat for those rougher winter climates. If you wear any kind of hat always remove it upon entering a place of business. This will show good manners and respect. When a person removes their hat it also represents openness and honesty. Not removing your hat can display a sense that you might be hiding something, or you are trying to disguise your true self. If you dress professionally, you will present yourself as an experienced businessperson, and customers will be more likely to discuss their requirements, needs and expectations.

Dress also depends on the type of market you are calling on. What type of culture are you trying to do business with? For example, if you are in the cattle business, you might be wearing jeans, cowboy boots and a hat. I have a close friend who is employed at the high corporate level of a semi-truck manufacturer. His position places him in the realm of owners, government officials, CEOs and CFOs. This person is responsible for selling fleets of semis around the globe. He told me while at the corporate office that he is expected to dress in tailored suits, white dress shirts, custom neckties and top of the line dress shoes. But when he is traveling internationally in today's fragile political climate, he dresses very casually so he will be inconspicuous, showing no company logos that may draw attention.

Today some business environments have become quite casual, but you will still need to determine when formal business attire is required. When you start dealing in large six to seven figure projects, formal business attire likely will be required.

Adjusting to cultural changes in your marketplace is crucial to creating a more relaxed business environment when you are attempting to form new business relationships or closing sales.

CHAPTER 24

Understand Your Pricing

In order to have profitable sales, you need to understand how the sell price is created. Understanding all the elements that make up your true cost is vital to achieving profitable business transactions.

I was dealing with a community college, and we were performing services on their air conditioning units. The machines were in a large mechanical room with windows exposing one wall to the campus grounds so the students could see the insides of the physical plant as they walked to their classes. The customer wanted us to accept their terms and conditions with our preventive maintenance program. Whenever this happens, we have our legal team determine if the customer's terms and conditions (T&Cs) are acceptable. What we found was that their T&Cs did not protect us against extenuating circumstances. They wanted us to be responsible for any damages that may occur during services on their AC units. For example, if a student was walking to class and looks over at our technicians working on a machine and stumbles and breaks his ankle, we would be totally liable for that student's medical bills. Needless to say, we rejected their terms and conditions and the customer ended up signing our T&Cs.

Extenuating circumstances can be overcome by purchasing an insurance policy to cover those items, but that is an added cost which will be added to your proposal. There are companies that are willing to take the risk of extenuating circumstances and then you will need to ask yourself if it's truly worth the risk to compete. Loss of production is another example of extenuating circumstance, and that risk could be in the millions of dollars. How much risk do you as a salesperson, or your company want to take? A company can go out of business over legal fees if sued by a customer over not complying with their T&Cs, losing huge sums of money over legal fees.

Technical advances and how they can be applied to performing sales functions can greatly assist you in increasing the closure of business. As I mentioned earlier, by using all the components that we have available, these technical advances reduce the amount of time to respond to a customer's needs and increase your ability to handle larger quantities of proposals and RFPs. A quick response shows the customer that you care about their time and that you are a person who does not waste time, but instead brings a sense of urgency to the request. As they say in the business world, "time is money". Another remarkable thing about the internet is the ability to research new prospects, learning how large their organization is, or finding out who the main players are that make the buying decisions. What is their true line of business? What do they sell and who are their customers? This is all useful information to have in your back pocket just in case during your conversations with the customer any of these topics arise. But don't get overjoyed by delivering all this accumulated information to your customer, you may come across as an arrogant know-it-all. How you converse is how you build your personal relationship with your customer.

Remember your customer spends a large amount of time at their workplace. Sometimes they may take pride in educating you about their company - this is how you can build personal connections and trust. Most people like talking about themselves, what they do or how important their position is. Let them talk all they want, and they will end up thinking you're a pretty nice person and remember people like to do business with people they like.

Do not spend all your time emailing customers, thinking you can close business that way. You are a salesperson, not some backroom person working the phones in a boiler room atmosphere. Make appointments, go out into the marketplace. This is where face-to-face contact is true and vital in building relationships. Remember the 'delete' button is quite easy to access, especially for the customer who has never seen you before. They may have heard about your company, but they can always contact your company through other avenues like calling your boss or upper management. You don't want this; you want your customers contacting you directly. You are representing your company and need to be the main point of contact for business.

Keep your emails as short as possible. Your customer does not have all day to read a historical dissertation. Short and to the point, hitting all the important items is a better avenue.

The larger the project, the larger the proposal will be. RFPs from government, utilities or major company projects can be very large, possibly multi-million-dollar transactions. Try thinking outside the norm. Be creative, offer something that your competitors cannot, show attributes only your company can offer and present them in a way that will save your customer money while providing a higher quality product and service. You can accomplish this by asking your customer questions such as: what shipping companies they prefer, can they set up on-site inventories, would they like ongoing operational training, what kind of guaranteed response times they would like to see. Perhaps let them know if your company does not respond within the required time on service calls, they can get a discount on the hourly rate or on the invoice amount. How many technicians are required to live within a determined mile radius from your service location? Use information such as this and differentiate yourself and your company from your competition, increasing your ability to win.

If the products you are marketing are the type that can be utilized by a broad range of customers, then your possibilities of creating new customers will increase. For example, at one time I was selling industrial hose products. I was driving on the interstate on my way to meet one of my customers and I passed a semi-truck pulling double pneumatic tanks which I learned later transport dry products such as flour, fertilizers or powdered cement. I got the trucking company's name off the driver's door as I passed. Then I contacted the company and asked for their mechanical shop and made an appointment with their shop manager. I was able to sell him hose and fittings that I had seen on their pneumatic tanker trailers. Taking it a step further, I researched that trucking industry and created a new market sector which over the years I sold all types of industrial products to such as specialized hoses, fittings, hose clamps, hose assemblies, reels of hose, pressure and temperature gauges, meters, and all types of industrial valves. Basically, by keeping your eyes open you can find different applications for the products you represent and market, increasing your sales and income.

Within our market area there were manufacturers of heavy equipment and products such as forklifts, semi-trucks, tanker trailers for those semi-trucks, food grade stainless steel tanks for the wine industry, pressure washers, plywood mills, lumber mills, paper mills, chemical plants and so forth. All these market segments have multiple vendor sand these business purchase components to keep their productions moving. If a single component such as a hydraulic, pneumatic, mechanical or a controls device fails, their production process can come to a halt and incurring tremendous financial losses. If their products are not being produced, then they are not making money. In the semiconductor or paper industries, they have backup machinery and systems in case a failure occurs, preventing a shutdown of production. There could be huge economic losses for a company, possibly into the hundreds of thousands or millions of dollars per hour or per day depending on the cost to produce their products. The idea I am trying to convey is that all around us there are opportunities to create new customers, markets and relationships. All a person needs to do is open their eyes and mind to those opportunities. Talk to people. Google is our friend. Websites give us valuable information so we can become knowledgeable about a business sector. What do they sell? How long have they been in business? Do they pay their bills? The world is your oyster - open it up!

When the time arrives for you to deliver your proposal or your RFP, the pricing you present to your customer will be the right price with the correct profit. Do your homework and your chances of closing the sales will be in your favor.

CHAPTER 25

Keep Good Records

Keeping records from your important communications, meetings, contracts won or lost, and purchase orders can be valuable when issues arise. When they do arise, and they will, the person with recorded documents can reveal what occurred saving time and money.

In the selling profession you need some strategy for keeping records, developing a system to organize how you address your market and your customers. Each person can create their own system of record keeping. For example, individual folders or files for each customer grouped or geographical areas, by counties or sites for different categories such as the paper industry, educational districts, food industry and so on. The main idea is to have a system where you can access their contact information quickly on customers accessing their titles, their history of orders placed, and buying cycles. Does the customer purchase weekly, monthly, quarterly, annually, or once every so often? When do they go out for RFPs?

Knowing these buying cycles is critical to being in the game. Keeping you ahead of your competition can increase your chances of closing more and larger sales. What does your customer expect from the winning contractor? How can you assist and influence your customer in creating an RFP that only your company can provide specific line items? The better relationship you have with your customers, the better chance you have in assisting and influencing the RFP's specifications around your company's products and services.

There was a large maintenance agreement that covered several commercial facilities throughout a metropolitan area. The HVAC company I was selling for at the time had six technicians living within a fifteen-mile radius from the customer, so I asked the customer to specify in the RFP that the bidder must have six factory trained technicians that live within that fifteen mile radius and must respond within two hours seven days a week to emergencies or there would be a monetary penalty. I had the customer add other specifications such as the winner of the RFP must stock original equipment manufacturer (OEM) maintenance items such as belts, filters and lubricants on site at the various facilities. When the bid opening day arrived, there were half a dozen bidders at the award meeting. I won the contract, which had a five-year term in the amount of six figures per year not including extra repair services.

The lesson of this story is, if you keep good records and know when the customer is going out for bids with their RFP, you will be aware of the schedule of events when your competitors are not. If you have been calling on the customer over a lengthy period, months or even years, creating good business and personal relationships with them you might be invited to assist in creating the specifications of the RFP giving you an advantage over your competition.

I used a business card holder for transferring customer information to my iPhone/laptop contact application. The business card folder gives a very quick visual of your customer contact names, titles, addresses, emails, phone and fax numbers, and your personal notes and observations. I can flip through the business card folder and immediately see names and companies so I can plan my business day. With an iPhone or laptop, you only see one item or page at a time. With an iPhone calendar you can be alerted on future appointments and customer bid dates.

I started scanning all my customer orders and POs into a desktop file, so I can easily access any history of a customer. I can see what was purchased, when, the cost, quantities, and most important who did the purchasing. With this information I can predict, to a certain degree, their buying cycles.

Management always wants to know what you're working on and what future business may occur. Being able to easily access your proposals and RFPs you have delivered and where they are in the closure process will save you time so you can concentrate your efforts on trying to close other sales. I never tell my management everything that I am working on because then they will put that information into their reports and expect you to close everything, trying to make themselves look like they are the ones responsible for the sales, which really is not the case. Part of the time you need to make them feel they're part of the selling process, so they feel they are a part of the big picture of what you are selling. When you do close a sale that they are not aware of, you get to surprise them and impress them with your ability to create that new business.

I have seen many very professional salespeople carry with them a journal tablet to every meeting, recording the date and time, names of persons attending with their titles, and taking notes from the meeting such as the discussion topics, decisions made, who is responsible for what, and scheduled events agreed upon. This is a fantastic way to review later in case any disagreement may arise. Once I knew a manager that met with a customer to discuss a critical interpretation of a contract and there was a group of people there. Unfortunately, the manager did not identify the persons present. One silent individual was a lawyer for the company who employed the manager who was arguing the interpretation of the service contract. The manager was later terminated from the company and one of the facts was breach of contract that was witnessed by that silent bystander. Lesson learned: identify the people present during meetings so you know who you are speaking with. They could be the owner, the CFO, CEO, or the janitor. Know who you are talking to. If you don't, it can come back and possible cost you if things start going wrong.

It's a good idea to take notes during meetings with customers. This shows respect for what your customer is saying. One time I was selling valves to a tanker trailer manufacturing company. My customer called me into a meeting with their customer. The valves were priced at $285 each and the order was for a quantity of 468 for a total sales cost of $133,380. Their Alaskan customer thought the price was too high. I checked the specifications of the valves and found that the valve gasket material was priced at $135 each and designed for petroleum applications. Their customer asked me if there was a less expensive gasket material that could handle petroleum products. I checked and found one that could handle the product for $50 each, saving the customer $35,100. He changed the order to reflect the lesser expensive gasket material, changing all 468 tankers with the new specified gaskets. Around six months later, after all the new petroleum trailer tankers were delivered, their Alaskan customer contacted the tanker manufacturer threatening a lawsuit because all the valves had seized in the closed position and were unable to operate due to the extreme cold winter temperatures. Because of that meeting six months earlier, the manufacturer and I had recorded the customer changing the gasket specification with his signature for the change order. This documentation proved that the Alaskan customer was at fault. The customer ended up placing a huge change order to the manufacturer to retrofit all the butterfly valves with the more expensive original specified gasket that could handle the subzero winter temperatures. That was the original reason for the higher priced gasket material. The lesson learned here is that by taking good notes and obtaining signatures of authorization for change orders can save you a possible lawsuit and many sleepless nights!

Sometimes salespeople end up in situations where their bosses are unexperienced or have no experience with sales or salespeople and want their sales team to record every phone call, every conversation, every scheduled meeting, every order won or lost and why, almost to the point of your every move needs to be recorded. This type of management only frustrates the sales teams and can cause difficult relations with the managers and their sales team. This, of course, is an example of micromanaging and is counter-productive to focusing on creating good business and strategizing on closing sales. The manager ends up with a huge amount of data that he will never have time to review. Call reports are good to show what the salesperson is working on and the dollar value of those sale targets. I never minded doing sales reports that summarized my sales calls in a quick, short format, but recording every minute communication and action is a ridiculous waste of time.

Lesson learned: record keeping is critical when it is related to the development of customers, creating good, knowledgeable business and closing profitable sales. It can be overkill in requesting excessive amounts of information however and can also be demoralizing and destructive to building a strong sales team. Let the professional salespeople do their job: sell.

At the end of the day, the person who has kept the best records can reference them in times of conflict, resolving problems, saving time, and closing stronger sales.

CHAPTER 26

Networking & Socializing is Good for Business

The importance of networking and socializing through industry associations and organizations should be a norm if you want to increase your business. Whatever you are representing, selling, or marketing I am sure there are associations and organizations that are related to your products or services. In the construction industry there are all types of supply businesses such as plumbers, HVAC suppliers, electricians, building supplies, steel workers, chemical supplies, engineering companies and so on. There are associations, organizations, and unions for all types of suppliers of products and services for all kinds of companies. There are trade shows happening during the year throughout the country for the many different industries. You need to be attending and participating in these industrial organization shows that you are selling to. For example, if your biggest customer is the medical care industry, each state has their own association (Oregon has OHSA, or Oregon Hospital Society of America) who answers to their national board that oversees each state for compliance with national codes and standards. Commercial real estate has a national organization called BOMA (Building Owners and Managers Association) that lobbies government for codes and standards in their industry. If you can become a member of such groups, you will be socializing with some of the main decision makers who you should be dealing with. I always made a point of having a vendor booth at their trade shows. This way you are investing in their industry by displaying your latest services and products. I have participated in these trade shows many times as a speaker discussing relevant topics or have been on panels answering questions concerning future changes such as the environmental regulations or the utilization of the current energy efficient retrofits, rebates and incentives.

While selling service and equipment in the HVAC markets, I made sure our company attended these trade shows. I would see many of my customers there along with specific decision makers who had issued purchase orders to me. I also met with subcontractors who have teamed up with me on projects. I was able to see what competitors attended and which ones did not attend. If possible, I always try to connect with the show organizers prior to the event to make sure we get a prime location for our booth to maximize our exposure.

You don't want your booth hidden in the back corner of the venue where few people pass by. A prime location for your booth would be in front by the main entrance with none of your competitors in sight. Sometimes having a friendly company at a neighboring booth can be to your advantage. The cost for all this is an investment towards the growth of your business. But of course, if the event is weak and has a small attendance, you may opt not to participate depending on how you analyze your return-on-investment cost for membership and a vendor booth. During these trade shows you can contact your product factory representative to get them involved. Sometimes a factory representative can assist you in the cost of the vendor booth and help you during the show by possibly discussing new products with customers as they visit the display booth. Whenever a customer visits your vendor booth and shows interest in your products or services get all their contact information and tell them you will connect with them within a week for an appointment to discuss the matter in further detail. If you make one to three sales from the trade show, you will have paid for the membership cost and/or the vendor booth and hopefully develop some long-term customers that can lead to larger sales in the future, strengthening your profit base.

In the industrial controls sector, there is ISA (Instrumentation Society of America) which focuses on process controls for all types of industries such as semi-conductor, water treatment, chemical processing, petroleum, food processing, wood products and paper products. ISA has their own membership, monthly local and regional meetings, educational programs and regional and national trade shows. Any type of market usually has an organization or association that lobbies government setting standards and codes. All you need to do is search the internet for the industry/market you are selling in and all the associations, organizations and their conferences can be accessed. You can also just ask your customers what organizations they belong. Some companies have full time personnel who attend all the related conferences and trade shows that are associated with their markets. Some of the largest trade shows in the country are the annual automotive show in Detroit and the annual high-tech show in Las Vegas. The lesson here is to get involved and participate in your industry's associations. You and your company will only benefit from this.

You can also differentiate your company and yourself by organizing annual customer seminars. Find a good facility with accommodating parking and lodging. Sometimes you can even utilize a friendly customer's facility. You can ask your customers what topics they would like to see covered and which would benefit them the most and try to incorporate those topics into the seminar's agenda. You can invite speakers who are experts in their field. In the HVAC industry the pumping of water is involved, so you could invite a major industrial pump company to participate as a speaker. There is electrical and natural gas power used in HVAC systems, so you could invite speakers from the local utilities to speak about the future of their industries. Energy usage is always a concern for facility managers, so invite a government specialist in the energy conservation field to present the different rebates and energy incentive programs that are available.

If the seminar is in the morning, you can provide fruit juices, coffee and pastries and at noon break into a buffet luncheon. During this time, the customers can interact with one another. The speakers can discuss the latest topics that directly affect your customers. You can have factory representatives and engineers speak about the latest advancements concerning components like cooling towers, electric variable frequency drives for HVAC motors. Schedule the seminar for a Friday, giving them a break from their five-day work week, making sure it ends by 3pm so the attendees can miss the end of the week traffic. Of course, there is a financial cost to arrange a seminar, but having many of your loyal customers in one place providing them with the latest information and giving them the opportunity to meet and socialize with other customers is priceless. You are thanking them for the long-term business by providing them with an educational experience. Don't just send out an email invitation, instead design an invitation and have them printed and mailed to each attendee, then follow up with each to confirm the number of people who will attend to make sure you have enough food, informational literature, and promotional items. Customer seminars, conferences, and trade shows are one of the best ways to network, socialize, meet new customers, and develop new business relationships. You never know who you may meet that can create a game-changing relationship, financially and personally.

Many times you will hear the question from sales trainers and managers, "who is your customer?". Salespeople usually respond by breaking up their markets into segments of product use such as hose and medical equipment, or they respond that the buyer is the customer. Philosophically, everyone is your customer because you never really know who you are speaking with. The person at the grocery store that you happen to encounter in the checkout line and have a conversation with about the latest flavors of ice cream could easily be the senior purchasing agent for a major company that has a need of your products and services. Therefore, EVERYONE is your customer and you are selling all the time. You are really selling yourself - remember, people like doing business with people they like.

When you are out in the marketplace or attending a trade show or conference you need to take advantage of networking and social environment if you want to grow your business and build stronger relationships.

CHAPTER 27

Find the Decision Maker

If you want to sell something you need to locate the person who has the authority and financial power to purchase.

A close friend of mine and I had a conversation about getting in front of decision makers. He was employed with a very large banking company and had worked in the personal accounts division representing trust funds and retirement accounts. He was attending one of their west coast sales meetings in San Francisco when one of their newer and upcoming sales associates was giving a presentation of how to capture new business. The person presenting based everything on the premise that an excellent presentation was the main key to capturing a potential customer, believing that a strong presentation would convince the potential customer to turn their financial trust and funds over to them to manage. My friend at this meeting raised his hand and asked the question, "yes, a good presentation is important, but tell me how did you get all those potential customers to attend your presentation?". The person was dumbfounded and couldn't answer.

The above story really happened. Don't get me wrong, presentations are important. But only if you have an audience that includes decision makers. You need to qualify your audience. Whether it be a maintenance manager, a plant engineer, an owner, or purchasing agent. You can just ask the simple question, "can you issue a purchase order?" and if by chance the person says no then ask them what their company's procedure is in purchasing orders, or who the person is in the company that issues purchase orders or signs agreements. This way you might be introduced to a person who has the authority to issue purchase orders or sign agreements. It is amazing sometimes the information you can obtain by just asking pertinent questions. It might feel uncomfortable, but if you wish to reach the person with the power to make buying decisions, you will need this information: Who does the purchasing?

Good questions and statements to ask are what types of services and products their company uses, how often do they require those types of components and services, what prices are they looking to spend on the components and services, can you inventory those items for them, have they thought about a multi-year agreement, etc. Be creative. Ask questions during your conversations with your customers. This way you will accumulate information that can assist you with your customers in future dealings.

Don't be wasting your time and energy or your customer's. Time is money. Use your time wisely while in front of buyers and decision makers. And, if you are going to be making presentations, make sure you have the correct people who can truly issue purchase orders or sign contracts.

CHAPTER 28

Use Your Intuitive Ability

The ability to use your intuitive attributes can be crucial to capturing successful business. That gut feeling to proceed or not can produce consequences which can be exceptionally good or disastrous.

Looking back on my career, remembering those moments when for some reason I made that phone call or turned onto a new street connecting with an opportunity that didn't exist previously, I felt that my intuition was directing me. It was a subconscious action taken in a relaxed state that seemed to always end in an interesting, even profitable, situation sometimes ending up connecting with a new customer or creating a new relationship. This is an example of an attribute that some salespeople have - a feeling of intuition. That gut feeling you get when you're out in the field making sales calls and you decide to stop at that business you have been driving by for months or even years and discover that they have a need for your products or services.

There was a very small chemical company down the road from a very good customer of mine. One day I stopped in at that company and introduced myself, and discovered they were using our equipment. I was introduced to the plant manager who was very friendly and kind. We connected, and she told me all about her home in Louisiana. She signed our service agreement for the equipment and a long-term business relationship started.

It never hurts to ask questions during these first meetings. How long have you operated out of this location? What type of customers do your products serve? Does your company have other locations? What purpose does our equipment have in relationship to your production?

Sometimes I ask a potential customer for the opportunity to prove ourselves. Of course you would first need an order to have that opportunity. Once you deliver on that first order and have proven yourself as a consistent, reliable person who represents a superior product and company, the customer may start using your services more often. Many times, a business relationship can start with that first order and can build over the years into a large, profitable business relationship.

Other times things just go wrong or turn out bad. Murphy's law states that sooner or later something will fail. It will happen - such as a late delivery, a faulty product or a poor service response. But this can be an opportunity to prove yourself as a responsive problem-solver for your customer. When a customer calls complaining about a problem with your company, they really are showing you that they respect the business relationship they have with you. They are giving you a chance to see how you will respond and solve their problem. It is when a customer doesn't contact you about a problem and just disappears that you need to worry. How you and your company respond to a customer's problem can make or break the relationship.

One time our parent company was having trouble with a large Japanese customer. Our product had a problem and the customer was about to change vendors. The amount of business involved was likely in the hundreds of millions of dollars. As soon as the news reached our CEO, he cancelled all his appointments, jumped into our corporate jet, flew directly to Japan, and met one-on-one with the CEO of that company.

The customer was "Japan Airlines", and the product was jet engines, and we were the only supplier for OEM parts and training. Our CEO made the necessary product and service adjustments for the customer, and they remained loyal to our company. The problem could have been a number of things, but the point is that our CEO addressed it personally and quickly.

Our CEO intuitively felt he needed to respond in person instead of delegating the problem to a subordinate. When you delegate something to someone else you are passing that responsibility away from yourself, and if that person fails they become the "scapegoat". Sometimes, if you want it done right you need to just do it yourself. Our CEO just knew somehow that he had better act quickly or that Japanese customer would be down the road building a new relationship with a competitor.

Following your intuition, that gut feeling, can create new relationships and learning experiences. Be aware of your surroundings because sometimes your intuition may want you to exit a situation, preventing a poor outcome. Information is power. Revealing a faulty specification can save the financial outcome of a project or increase your credibility. If you believe revealing information can help a situation, share it and if you feel the information may raise unnecessary questions with prolonged time-wasting discussions that can lengthen the closing process of the sale, then try to be focused only on that which is relevant to the sale. The old saying, "less said, best said" can be applied in many business discussions. For example, profit margins are almost always best withheld. An exception would be an agreed profit margin between a buyer and the seller prior to the purchase.

The above business situations all have a factor of intuition. When all the specifications and calculations for a proposal or RFP are completed and ready for final review prior to delivery someone may ask how you feel about the pricing, or do you feel you can close the sale. The main idea is to deliver on what the RFP or proposal requests and then add a little something extra - a creative item, a new way to meet and beat the expectations of the customer and surpassing your competition. Your customer may even reveal to you what your chances are of closing the sale when they see your new creative features.

Intuitive feelings can also be feelings of fear or failure. We can only try to look at all the possibilities that may occur and then move on. Another saying, "nothing ventured, nothing gained" comes to mind. I have my own personal saying about failed situations, "if I learned from all my mistakes, I should be a genius by now". So keep moving forward using those intuitive feelings to better your advantage in closing more business.

CHAPTER 29

Communicate With Your Customers

In life just as in business communicating to your customers, your team and management is crucial to having successful outcomes. When communicating with customers you must also remember to listen carefully to what they are saying. It is a two-way street. At the end of a business meeting I often do a quick summary to verify that I understand what was discussed and agreed upon to make sure everyone is on the same page and moving in the same direction.

A good friend of mine who's been selling professionally for most of his career told me of a multi-million dollar negotiated sale concerning a municipal airport and the installation of a solar panel farm on the vacant acreage on the grounds surrounding the runways. Both parties had come to agreement and the customer wanted to move forward on the solar project. The only thing left to do was to process the paperwork, so upper management pulled my friend from the project and directed him to concentrate on other potential sales. The so-called minor details of the closing paperwork were delegated to another member of the company. My friend was getting copied on the project's emails and thought everything was moving along smoothly. After about four months had passed, the airport solar farm customer called my friend informing him that he was about to back out of the project because their finance calculations had changed on what they would need to invest in the project. The customer was quite upset because he had not heard anything about the situation from my friend's company in over three months. During that telephone conversation my friend spent two hours trying to persuade the customer that his company could provide the necessary funding to ensure that the project could move ahead, solving the customer's financial problem. He tried to assure the customer that he would be the main point of contact from then on. The customer liked the salesman and due to their good relationship, he conveyed that he was about to retire in a few months and really wanted this project to be part of his legacy.

You're better off just closing a sale yourself instead of delegating the responsibility to a team member. Also, when entering a multi-million-dollar project, the customer should be given personal attention. When the person who was delegated to finalize and close the sale ran into difficulties with the customer, they should have contacted my friend who was the person who originated the relationship with the customer. That way he could address the problem at that time instead of three months later when it was too late.

Having to do damage control could have been averted if the communication had been better between the members of the sales team. My friend's company was even presenting the project as being closed and booked. They had touted how great the project would be for the company. They lost the contract; nothing was ever signed and the solar farm at the airport didn't happen.

Remember, stay close to your customers and communicate. Listen and follow through personally until you have a purchase order or signed contract.

CHAPTER 30

Have a Positive Attitude

Most people don't like being around negative people. If you present all the poor qualifies of your products and service, do you think customers would genuinely want to purchase from you? Not likely. People and buyers like doing business with persons who present themselves with a can-do attitude.

There exists an upper level of selling that has always interested me. Those people who sell the seven to nine figure deals and who are mostly employed with fortune 500 corporations, deal makers in commercial real estate or possibly transactions involving purchasing professional sport franchises in the NBA or NFL. Someone somewhere is doing these deals, bringing people together to consummate an offer and acceptance into agreement. The entrepreneurs of the world grow their business. Several classmates of mine from college became highly successful businesspeople. One started a structural wood glue lamination architectural company and ended up employing over a hundred and fifty people. Another classmate started a high-end real estate residential property management company with support for private boutique hotels at resort locations like Park City, Utah, Whistler Ski Resort in British Columbia, Jackson Hole in Wyoming, and other prime resort locations. These successful classmates had one thing in common, they came from families who had a strong business and entrepreneur background.

Of course there is always the exception like the immigrant who came to this country with nothing and after years of arduous work and taking financial risks compiled an economic empire. Bill Gates and Paul Allen, both college dropouts, with their intellect and vision created Microsoft.

It was one of those weeknights in the winter of 1971 and I was a student at Washington State University studying late at the library. After the library closed, I walked over to the student union building and joined friends for a late-night cup of coffee. We were all seated around the table talking about professors, exams, music and whatever topics arose until the cafeteria closed and we had to return to our dormitories (or in my case a fraternity). While at the table, I was introduced to a guy by the name of Paul who was studying computer science. He had a very thick burly beard and was a calm and pleasant person. He lived in one of the fraternity houses further down the hill from the campus. Since we were headed in the same direction, we walked down the hill together into the Greek section. I can't remember what we talked about, probably what it was like living in a fraternity, but we parted when we reached my house. It was many years later I realized that Paul, who I met at the student union cafeteria that evening was Paul Allen, one of the founders of Microsoft. I had read his autobiography and realized by the description of the fraternity and timeframe that he was indeed that same Paul I had met that night. The learning point to this story is that you never know who you are speaking with or who you will encounter during your normal day.

There is an old saying, "the proof is in the pudding", meaning the results tell the story. Closing business, capturing orders and contracts is the proof of a successful salesperson. With me, I had to succeed to provide for my family, trying to give them the best possible life. I started selling in the late seventies and early eighties during a rough recession. The economic climate of that time tested my selling ability. If you can sell enough to cover your cost and make profits for your company in poor economic times, then in a good economic environment you should prosper. In economic recessions a good business/salesperson will create their own economy.

There are a lot of words that describe a good salesperson: persistent, curious, creative, personal, consistent, punctual, honest and attentive to name a few. Some descriptions can be negative: dishonest, obnoxious, loud, flamboyant, arrogant, pushy, etc. I have always tried to think of myself on the positive side.

One of my favorite sayings about selling is that you must balance your relationship with your customer between being obnoxious and persistent. I had a customer who I was trying to close a large five-figure sale with, providing an energy retrofit for a 300-horsepower compression motor, and I was dealing with the Department of Energy of Oregon at the state capital in Salem. They were taking their time and delaying the project. The customer wanted the state to confirm the rebate payment on the project prior to issuing the purchase order. It took me six weeks to finalize the rebate payment with the state and secure the documentation. During that time, I called the customer after each meeting with the state energy rebate people to make sure he was aware of the status on rebate which represented a 50% portion of the project.

One morning my manager received a phone call from the customer complaining about all the phone calls from me on the status of the state's energy rebate payment. The customer said I was bothering him by all the phone calls. Fortunately for me, my manager was gracious and understanding enough to tell him that I was just doing my job. We received the purchase order for the project during that telephone call. Sometimes when you think you are doing the right thing by keeping your customer informed you may be unaware that you might be overdoing it. Sometimes it is too much, and other times are not enough. It becomes the old balancing act. But the more time you spend actively selling and creating business with new customers, the better you become at determining what is too much and what is too little with your customers. As I previously mentioned, use your intuition. I try to put myself in my customer's shoes. I try to become part of their team. If you can become part of their business team connected with their profit and loss functions, their trust and loyalty towards you will increase. Another saying that comes to mind is, "take care of those who take care of you" and things will work out for the best.

In order to make things happen, you must be doing those things that cause things to happen. This may sound a little nutty and simple, but I believe it is true. I have often said when business slows down that something always comes along. A phone call from out of the blue or an old customer has just gotten approval on a large project you have been working with him for months on, or you stop by a new customer who suddenly has a need for your services. Intuition: one day you feel you should call some old contact and suddenly things start in motion towards an order. It is a real high closing good profitable business. I have even caught myself doing a happy tap dance celebration in my office on a few occasions.

Don't give up. Have a positive attitude. Keep contacting as many customers as you can. Stay organized and use your intuition, and things will work out for the best and your sales will start increasing. Someone said that there are three types of people: those who make things happen, those who watch things happen, and those who wonder what happened. Which one do you want to be?

CHAPTER 31

Complete the Sale

From the first meeting, through the offer and acceptance, to the purchase order and receiving payment for services delivered is the cycle of the sales process. Of course, each sales is unique to itself. As previously mentioned, capturing the order, the contract, the purchase order, the all-important signature to proceed is the acceptance of your offer. This is so critical - you need the ink, the signature, to manifest a sale. I have experienced so many times when people move ahead on something even when there is no purchase order or a signed agreement and the trouble this causes can be horrific, landing you in legal proceedings, out-of-pocket money or even loss of employment. I don't know how many times I heard someone say "I have the order" and then ask them if they have a purchase order or signed agreement and they get upset because they don't. The fact of the matter is if you don't have a signature or PO, you don't have anything. I might be hard on this topic, but I don't know how many times management starts congratulating themselves and start celebrating prior to closing the sales or receiving the signed contract and discovered later that they lost the contract to their competitor. Close the sale first, then you can celebrate. Better yet, celebrate after you have received the final payment!

Examples of closing statements:

- If we can provide this product at this price, would you be willing to move ahead?
- If there isn't anything else you need concerning the product, then all we need is a purchase order so we can proceed.
- We can deliver the product at the date and price you liked, all I need is permission to proceed by way of a purchase order or signature on my proposal.

There are numerous types of closures to a sale. Each salesperson has his or her own personal style. Some of the important things about becoming a successful salesperson is having good personal manners like politeness, listening skills, being sincere, showing empathy and conversational skills are good traits to possess. Be courteous and polite.

When I first started selling, I thought anybody could make a living as a salesperson. I discovered later that not too many people can, and most would never think of being a salesperson as a lifetime occupation. You need that salesperson personality. A lifelong friend of mine who is the nicest and most wholesome person you could ever meet was between jobs looking for employment. I introduced him to a local company looking for a salesperson and they offered him the position. My friend ended up leaving the position - it just wasn't his cup of tea. After about one year he went back to his old employer as a metal fabricator. My friend had a 'B' personality type, more of an introvert and probably felt uncomfortable having to meet new people and asking for the orders. But there are a few people with 'B" personality types who excel in the selling profession. They use what I call the "quiet close". These salespeople are so relaxed and calm that the buyer starts to feel comfortable and not pressured to buy, and then starts to feel he can trust this person to deliver on his requisitions. There always seems to be an exception to the rule. One day you think you have it all figured out and then you meet someone, or a new occurrence happens and you feel the need to rethink your ideas and assumptions.

Don't judge a book by its cover. Everyone has a hidden talent or something in their makeup that makes them special and unique. Everyone has something to offer.

CHAPTER 32

Proof Your Proposals

With today's technical advancements, business moves at a very quick pace. As with technologies, proposals can be created on the spot and delivered moments after they have been finalized. It is very important to always proof your proposals for any errors in grammar, spelling, calculations, making the necessary corrections. You want your proposals to look as professional as possible. You can access a customer file, retrieve a past proposal, edit the old proposal to reflect the requirements of the new proposal, rename it, and deliver it; and if possible, in person to make sure you have all the requirements addressed. This way you can try to close the sale at the time of delivery. You have the decision maker in front of you; no better time than the present to ask for the order. This will save you and your customer a lot of valuable time, giving you both more time to work on other projects.

Completing the sales is what business is all about. You need a purchase order or a signed contract to finalize a sale. Then you can move on to deliver what you sold.

The Spell Check Incident: There was a good customer of mine when I was in the water chiller business by the name of Precision Castparts. We needed to have the piping system for their process chilled water system redesigned so we could perform a high-level maintenance procedure. I contacted an engineer friend who I had used on many of our projects and introduced him to my customer the plant engineer. My friend was awarded the project to redesign the piping system. The day came when he completed the redesign report along with the necessary mechanical drawings. My engineer friend was running his report through the spell check before sending it to the customer. Unfortunately, the engineer was in a hurry and not paying attention during the spell check and just kept hitting the correction button without looking at the newly corrected words. On the cover page of the report was the customer's company name "Precision Castparts". "Castparts" is not in the English dictionary and came up as a misspelled word. The engineer hit the spell check correction key and replaced the word with whatever word the spell check used for the correct spelling replacement. The engineer finished the process of spell checking and faxed the document to the customer. What the title page showed was not "Precision Castparts" but instead showed "Precision *Castration*"! The mistake was discovered soon after the engineer had faxed the report and he quickly called the customer to notify them of the error. Luckily, the customer had a good sense of humor!

Lesson learned, proof your documents carefully or have someone look over it prior to sending it out, preferably delivered in person.

During my last tenure of employment, I sold energy saving programs where the customer would receive up to 50% or more of the cost of an approved energy saving project. The two types of energy sources we studied were electricity using units of kilowatts per hour (KWh) and natural gas energy in units of "therms". I had a large corporate customer and their North American headquarters had multiple opportunities for energy saving projects. One project was performing energy upgrades on one of their large commercial electrical water chiller compressors. To make an energy savings incentive payment on a project such as this, an engineer needed to perform a study on the operating energy usage of the electrical compressor to determine the best possible retrofit/upgrade to show the electrical savings. We hired an approved energy engineer to perform the study. When the study was completed, we would review the report to determine the best energy savings retrofit. I received the report first to see how much the KWh savings were on the water chiller compressor and what the return-on-investment time would be. The first thing I looked at was the amount of KWh saved. We were paying the customer twenty-five cents per KWh saved on approved energy studies. What I saw shocked me somewhat. The compressor on the water chiller had a 250-horsepower electric motor, therefore the energy savings should be in KWh, but instead it showed the energy savings in "therms" as if the motor used gas as its source of energy. The engineer and I had a long-term relationship with this customer. In fact, it was the engineer's largest account - his 'cash cow'. I brought this energy study to the engineer and paid him a good amount of money for a quality study. Therefore, I did not contact him to make the correction on the wrong source of energy. Instead, I let him present his study to the customer at the meeting I was present at as well. When the therms/KWh error was exposed by the customer, the engineer blew it off as a typo, but really it showed that he did not take time or make the effort to proof the document.

Lesson learned: Proof your work! Or have someone proof it for you and you will not look like a goofball and lose credibility with your customer.

One of my colleagues used the same engineer on an energy study for a fifteen-story commercial office building. When the report was completed and delivered to the customer, the front cover had a photograph of the wrong office building that was to be studied. You could only see a small portion of the top roof of the correct building that received the energy study. Again, a mistake was made reflecting poor attention to details by the engineer. The content of the study may have been excellent but having the wrong building on the front cover puts everything else into question. This is an example of haste makes waste! An extra few minutes, hours, days or however long it takes to make a report free from errors is time worth spending. Again, the report likely was not delivered in person. A goal of a salesperson is to be as professional as possible.

Another time I was visiting with a good customer who was employed by one of the largest property management companies in the area. He showed me an energy engineering report he had just received. He turned to one of the ages describing the building's HVAC system. The font was so small you literally needed a magnifying glass to read the information. Once again, the engineer who performed the study did not take time to proof or inspect the document prior to sending it to his customer, showing lack of concern for the customer and reflecting a lack of concern for professionalism. As stated before, take your time. Look over your work carefully before you present it to your customer so you will appear as a person who cares.

CHAPTER 33

Relationships Are What Its All About

Yes, having good relationships in our lives can bring much joy and can bring us financial security. As we travel through our daily lives and interact with those around us, whether they are our spouses, parents, children, siblings, teachers, managers, teammates or our customers, the quality of those relationships will at those moments determine how pleasant and enjoyable the outcomes will be.

I have a love and hate relationship with technology concerning the selling profession. I live with the fact that with today's technology you can organize your business day much more easily and accumulate useful information on your market than ever before, helping you make good business decisions. You can create customer files for accessing history on their projects and orders. When a new project appears their order files are at your fingertips and by editing an older proposal you can create a new proposal for a quick delivery. You may notice that I seem to be always looking for ways to increase efficiencies. As the saying goes, time is money. The more time you save, the more customers you can spend time with. This is a balancing act only you as a salesperson can achieve during your workday. An easy and quick guide to how well you spend your time during the workday is reflected in the amount of business you bring through the door. If you are managing your time correctly you will be closing orders while working on future business. That future business is what I call target customers - the ones you do not have yet but are trying to make them part of your customer base. Find the time to make appointments and meet with those target customers so you can start building new relationships. These new customers are the ones who will sustain and grow a business.

The bad part of technology is that it can make business impersonal. You cannot build a relationship with your customers if they never see you in person. The handshake, the smile, a chuckle, a raised eyebrow, or a frown cannot be emulated in an email or text. Personalities aren't expressed. Body language cannot be observed. Personal stories cannot be exchanged. Conversations about pricing, business environment, economics or employment status cannot occur unless you are meeting in person. Don't let the laptop take over your sales. Schedule appointments and go see your customers. If you aren't seeing your customers, your competitors most likely are and then you may start wondering why you are suddenly losing some of your good accounts.

Technology today with all the contact files, customer files, word documents, the ability to scan documents, emails and texting all used efficiently can give you an advantage in closing more sales. The reality today is that you can skype a meeting with a customer when you cannot meet in person. A company can create virtual reality (VR) tours of their facilities and personnel, but meeting in person will never be overcome by VR.

Several years ago, there was an airlines advertisement on television where in a conference room meeting with all the sales staff the company president stated they had a decrease in business and had been losing some of their top customers. The president blamed the decrease to too many faxes and emails. He then proceeded to hand out airline tickets to everyone in the conference room so they could visit in person those customers and discuss with each one what went wrong and what changes were needed to rebuild their confidence and secure the business relationship.

A close relative of mine has been in the banking industry in the personal banking sector dealing with trust funds, company assets and large money management investing for his whole professional career. I ask him with all the technology advances in communications, how often does he meet face to face with his customers. He said all the time. This made me feel hopeful that the face-to-face business time is alive and thriving. You can have a relationship over the web, but sooner or later you will need to meet your customer in person to truly keep and build the relationship to a higher level of trust and loyalty.

My last employer had a salesperson who only used emails to contact new potential customers with long, drawn out messages. One day he contacted me for a luncheon appointment. He told me that his sales numbers were so bad that the company had him on a performance program and he felt termination was soon to follow. If he didn't show some measurable improvement soon, he would become part of the unemployed sector of society. During our lunch he asked me for my advice on what he should do differently. To me it was simple. I told him to get out of the office and start knocking on potential customers doors, as many doors as possible and as soon as possible. To me it is a simple numbers game. The more doors you knock on, the ore chances you are going to run into someone who has a need for your products and services. A few months passed and his sales numbers started increasing to a point where he was removed from the performance plan. I congratulated him on his successful sales increase. He told me he just did what I advised him to do and started staying out of the office, concentrating on seeing as many potential customers as he could. I have caught myself while in the office stating to other salespeople, "do you see anyone in this office who can sign a purchase order or contract?", of course not. Because those people who can sign POs and contracts are out in the marketplace, not in your office.

When you are face-to-face with a customer, you learn about them, their hobbies, families and sometimes their troubles, just as they learn about you. This exchange of personal feelings, emotions and personalities is a building block of creating a relationship around trust, loyalty, and respect. A personal saying of mine is, "you need to give respect to get respect". Most people like to hear themselves talk. So let them talk! Others can be less talkative and may have a lot on their minds dealing with their daily responsibilities. My advice is to relax and listen carefully, sometimes the information revealed and exchanged can be the beginning of a long-term business relationship. Once I receive an order from a customer, I always try to do my best to deliver and follow, and confirm that the customer is satisfied with the outcome. Once the project is accomplished, I will return and try to repeat the process, capturing more orders as time passes.

There are times when out of nowhere the customer may want you to be involved with his company's business plan. Those smaller orders you have been dealing with might turn into large six figure projects when he invites you to the big party with an RFP. Other times your customer may give you unwelcome news like he is being transferred out of state or that their company has been purchased by their competitor and their operation is being shut down. Your customer might give you information about your competition, showing you their proposals or contracts revealing their weak points and possibly revealing their pricing. I know that showing a competitor's proposal or pricing is unethical, but let's get real - it happens more than we realize. When a customer shows me my competitor's proposal and pricing it is a great compliment of trust and loyalty. They want to keep me and my company as their primary vendor of services. They are telling me that they like us and are going to keep giving us their business. On occasions the opposite may occur because if they are showing me their pricing and proposals, they might be showing mine to my competitor and playing us against each other. Emails cannot get you this type of valuable information that can help you and your company make good decisions. Once an email is sent, it is out there for the whole world to access, and who knows how that might come back to harm you and your company.

An engineer friend of mine who works for a large successful engineering factory representative firm told me a story about one of their salespeople who had been trying for over a year to get an RFP from a large contractor. One day a new, older salesperson was hired. On their first day of employment that new salesperson had an RFP from that large contract faxed to him along with their competitor's proposal and pricing. Later that afternoon a six-figure contract was issued to his new company. By hiring this older, experienced salesperson who had strong business relationships in the market, the company increased their sales and customer base. Of course, there was a reason why that older salesperson left his last place of employment and moved to his new employer. Likely, he was being treated poorly due to a possible change in management. The offer from the new company may have included higher commissions or just a better working environment all around, possibly including increased vacation days, a signing bonus, or stock options. Whatever the reasons, they were enticing enough for him to leave his old employer. Stability and consistency of salespeople is difficult when changes are occurring with your company and in the marketplace. When management loses their salespeople, they have forgotten the importance of the relationships between their sales team and their customers.

Face-to-face personal contact with customers will help you know where you stand in that relationship. Get out of your office and go see customers! Schedule appointments and develop your craft and your style of selling. Be creative, show them someone who is unique. As the saying goes, "knock and the door will open". You may need to knock on several doors, but eventually one will open.

CHAPTER 34

The Three Land Mines of Selling

1. Religion: Religion is just too sensitive and personal to bring up in a conversation with your customers. Religion belongs outside the business environment. Of course, you will run into it during your business day with fellow employees and customers. If your customer brings up religion during a conversation, I usually listen sympathetically with a positive note of understanding, even if I disagree with some of their statements. I tend to respect the opinions of others too much to have an argument, especially about religion. I am there to do business, capture an order and create a relationship. Luckily, when I was a young man, I spent time in Rome visiting the Vatican and was exposed to the Roman Catholic religion. During that time, I was also in Oxford, England and was invited to a Christian seminary for the evening sermon. I would use these experiences as talking points for conversation when the Christian religion would become a topic with a customer.

Through my life I have noticed that those persons who were most quiet about their faith were the most religious. It always seemed to me that they would show evidence of their faith through their deeds, how they treat people and their ability to empathize. I feel it is best never to bring up religion as a topic of conversation. By chance if your customer does bring up religion as a topic, they might be opening a door to strengthening the relationship by revealing a personal part of their character. If this occurs, I feel it is best to listen with an understanding and agreeable ear. Remember, your customer has given their time from their busy workday to meet with you and may have a need to express a feeling about a part of their faith. This is a touch time if this happens. It could lead to a stronger relationship, increasing your chances of closing future business with them. The customers who have their Bible on their desk along with a crucifix hanging on the wall sometimes can be difficult to deal with, so be observant and cautious. For some reason I look quite conservative and have been known to come across as a very religious person, which is fine with me. The spiritual parts of a person should be private. If a customer feels relaxed and comforted by your views, that is a good thing.

My advice about religion as a topic of conversation with customers is to be cautious and sincere, and things should work out on the pleasant side.

2. *Politics:* Politics is just a big no-no. For sure it always seems to raise its ugly head. Personally, I don't like politics because I feel it divides people. When it comes to that topic of discussion it seems to me that people have their own opinions, and they feel theirs is the correct opinion. I read somewhere that Neil Young was on a musical tour during the time Ronald Reagan was running for the presidency. While on his tour bus, two Associated Press reporters interviewed Young. The reporters presumed that since he was part of the musical tour group *Crosby, Stills, Nash & Young* that he would be totally negative towards Reagan. They asked him his opinion of Reagan and expected to get a poor comment about Reagan's actions. Instead, Neil said he had never met the man so he couldn't make any kind of comment or judgement. The article that came out the next day stated Neil Young was a supporter! After that, Neil avoided any kind of interviews.

When politics appear in business meetings with customers, again I usually never disagree but listen politely with an understanding ear. The workplace is also a challenging environment to deal with political topics. I don't like political discussions, and they seem to always pop up. Most people have their minds already made up and have their views solidified. I heard a politician once make the statement, "we don't want to be like those Western Europeans". The first thought that came to my mind was that he probably had never been to a European country. Denmark for many years was rated the happiest country in the world and last year Finland beat them out and is now the happiest. I think that his arrogance, ignorance, and economic status blinded his perception of that part of the world. Whether your customer is a liberal, conservative, socialist or whatever, respect their point of view and listen politely. If you do make comments, be careful what you say. You are there to create business, not to debate and argue.

There was a cartoon posted on the wall of an office of a good customer of mine that showed a duel between two eighteenth century gentlemen. One being short and falling to the ground wounded while the other with his smoking pistol stood over his victim. The caption read, "don't win the argument and lose the sale". This is what can happen when politics enters business meetings or conversations. The lesson here is that you are better off avoiding politics as a topic of conversation with your customer. Try talking about fishing, sports, weather, music, traffic, a hobby, the latest holiday, kids, etc. - anything but politics. If you do want to talk politics, do it at your local watering hole.

3. Money: Money is a strange topic. Some people think price is a main part of the buyer's decision process. Many studies show that is not the case, but instead it is only a small part of the decision process for buyers. Price should be the very last topic to finalize the sales process. For example, there are some variables that affect the pricing of the product and/or services to be delivered such as over-time labor, travel expenses, delivery schedules, bonuses, or penalties for not meeting or beating the completion date of a project, payment schedules, special product details required, etc. When involving international agreements, foreign exchange rates on the value of the approved currency for the payments of the products involved is a major topic of discussion. Another subject is the location of the services to be performed. Will the customer provide transportation and lodging as part of the pricing? Does the customer take possession at the shipping source or at the delivery location? These factors are part of the pricing negotiation. For example, response time to a service call, local support inventory or access to the work site are also points of discussion that can be negotiated and can affect the pricing. Being all inclusive with these items will assist the buyer in making a buying decision.

Money of course is a status measurement. It always bothered me when people start talking about what they paid for this or that. I am happy they were able to make a good purchase. Seems like they are just wanting to show how good their negotiating skills are or how lucky or fortunate they were to make a good purchase. During the last recession the real-estate market collapsed, people were losing their homes. Looking closer at those who had lost their homes, you find some of them should never have had the mortgage approved in the first place based on their income. Someone who has a $60K annual income cannot afford a $500K home mortgage. At that time lenders were approving mortgages to anyone that was standing upright and breathing. The sell price meant little to the lender. The buyer got stuck back when the recession hit.

With money, talk is cheap. The more they talk, the less they usually have. I feel money is a very private thing. I have a close friend whose father was a successful contractor worth several millions of dollars. But to see him in public, he would appear as a local farmer dressed in bib-overalls and working boots. My friend said that his father purposely dressed like this because he did not want anyone to know just how wealthy he really was, fearing if they knew about his wealth, they would be hounding him to buy their wares.

When dealing with a customer concerning a purchase, questions usually arise concerning the timing of the delivery and the quantities required. I hate when a customer wants a cost right then and there during a meeting on something that is complex and requires a lot of calculations with multiple variables. I do my best to come up with a cost at that time and then tell them that every time this type of pricing request happens, I usually find myself giving pricing that is low. If you find yourself in a situation where you are put on the spot to give a price, try to give a high number so when you present your final price, hopefully it will be lower with a good profit margin. Be cautious when your customer requests a cost, or better yet just ask them what they would like to spend and then say you will do your best to hit that cost.

With larger, multi-million-dollar sales for service contracts, commercial products or real estate negotiations, legal discussions and internal political approvals may take months to even years to finalize the offerings and receive a signed agreement. The lesson learned is use your time wisely when creating your final proposed pricing. When a price is too low you can lose your shirt or even your job. It is better to price for profit and secure your future. Stay close to your customer during the buying process to complete the sell.

CHAPTER 35

The Importance of Being Prepared

This sounds so simple, being prepared. But the more prepared you are emotionally, physically, and intellectually, the better the chances are your customer will see you as someone that takes the time to do his homework and makes that extra effort to present accurate and knowledgeable information.

I have often told people that selling is a 24/7 occupation. Your job doesn't stop at 5pm. You will catch yourself lying in bed thinking about a new customer, how you should approach them with a new product, how to modify your pricing to hopefully capture an order, or what is the best way to present new features and benefits on a product. On occasion, while mowing the lawn or driving, I would start thinking of a novel approach to dealing with a business situation and discover a new way to beat my competition. You might find yourself thinking as if you were your customer and how best to assist his business, increasing their profits. When I was selling gauges to a controls panel manufacturer, I discovered that we could provide the gauge face with their company logo. Using this one selling experience I was able to increase our market share by providing OEMs with their own private logos on the face of their control panel gauges.

Think of your market in terms of what new customers you can develop by being aware. Keep your eyes and ears open. What new applications can your services or products be applied to? I call it exploring the marketplace. You never know if your services or products have a need until you ask. Prepare yourself, your day, your week, your month, your year and look out into the future asking yourself what is coming down the road. Plan and create new ways to attack your market. I use the term 'attack' because as they say, it's a jungle out there! For survival, you need to be the fittest and best prepared so you can stay employed and make a decent living.

Throughout my career I have used the term 'target'. I would sit down every Monday morning and make a target list of customers that I should contact to see if there was any potential business brewing. On that list would be customers who have given me orders in the past and who I had not seen or heard from in a while. Sometimes those are the customers who may issue an order quickly. Other times my intuition would tell me who to put on the target list. It's like a brainstorming procedure. Also on the list are companies I may have never been to that I want to introduce myself to, discovering what their status is concerning my products and learning what their place is in the business community and who are their customers. I put on the list big companies like Nike, Boeing Weyerhauser, Intel, Microsoft or Apple who might use my products regularly.

These customers should be put on a recurring schedule. At the end of the day, week or month, look over your list and see how many have been contacted and what were the outcomes. This target list is personal, and it will help you stay on track, focused, and assist your strategies to close more sales. After a while you will get a feeling for your rate of closing sales. Keep track of all the people you meet at these large companies because some will be a waste of time while others are decision makers. These decision makers are the ones you need to contact on a regular basis.

Being prepared also falls into the realm of your physical appearance. If you show up for an important appointment with a client and your dress is not appropriate, mud on your shoes with bad breath and wearing a stained or wrinkled shirt, smelling of alcohol with your hair uncombed, your chances of doing business that day or any day will be drastically diminished along with chances of remaining employed. Obtaining information on your customers is important. You should give your customer the opportunity to tell their own company stories and information. With today's technological sources for information at your fingertips like google, you can access massive amounts of information on a customer. But as I have mentioned previously, don't overdo it because you want the ability to ask questions so your customer can educate and inform you of some of the possible surprising facts about their company and themselves.

Preparation of your physical appearance and body language deserves to be touched upon again. Your posture reflects yourself. If you enter a customer's office with a shuffling stride, shoulders hunched and a frown on your face, or you look like a person with little confidence in your abilities to follow through on your commitments, chances of doing any business will be drastically diminished. If you enter a customer's office or a conference room of decision makers with a smile of sincerity, walking with a straight posture, shoulders back and chin up, the impression you create would be of a person with a sense of authority, an air of confidence who can be trusted. I was in a lobby of a well-known local company and on the wall was a plaque stating, "If you enter this office, please enter with a smile.". What a great statement! A simple smile can be a mood changer, a positive starter for a first encounter. Sometimes in the morning while preparing for my workday I would stand in front of the bathroom mirror and just smile for a while trying to set a positive mood in my mind for the coming day I have a close friend who has a degree in psychology. He told me a story about a clinical study performed at a major university where they took a large group of people diagnosed with depression and had them stare at the ceiling, smiling for ten minutes every morning prior to starting their day for a one-month period. The study revealed that after a month their depression started declining. A conclusion might be that feelings of happiness can increase by just smiling more. People like doing business with people who are in good spirits. A simple smile can set the stage for a good business relationship. Presenting your body language in a positive way will help you develop a strong first impression with your customers.

Preparing yourself psychologically, physically and intellectually before venturing out into the business world may give you that extra edge over your competition.

CHAPTER 36

Request for Proposals (RFPs)

Preparing proposals for customers is a critical time in the process of closing sales. Most companies use proposal/quote forms with the company's standard terms and conditions (T&Cs) attached, so when you create RFPs, the T&Cs become part of the agreement. Proposal forms should show information such as your company address and company name along with the company logo, phone and fax numbers and website. The terms and conditions are critical if things start going sideways or disagreements arise during the sales process. One element of the T&Cs shows the limitations of the warrantees. As an example, the servicing company will be responsible for their workmanship and will pass on all factory warranties such as on OEM parts. But the servicing company will not warranty or be responsible for extenuating circumstances such as loss of production profits or losses due to acts of God like tornadoes, earthquakes, or floods.

A proposal should have an introduction section and then a section listing numerically or with bullet points what your company will be providing. Just as important as what is being covered by your company, you should always list what is not covered. A good statement to use is: "Anything not listed above will be addressed separately". This way the customer can add or delete items which will affect the pricing accordingly. After listing the items that are included and not included, I would make the following separate statement:

Your cost for the above-described services/products is $$$$

Accepted   by: ___________________________________

Date: _______________________

Purchase   Order

#____

____

This way when you deliver your proposal in person the buyer can sign and or issue a PO number right then. If he wants to make any adjustment to your proposal, they can be made then on the document with the buyer's initials and current date by the adjustments.

The sell price is a topic that hopefully will finalize a sale. Use it in a closure statement such as, "if this price works for you, then all we need to move ahead is your signature or a PO.". Hopefully you have already agreed on the price and now it should be only a formality and the last step in the selling process. If you receive a signature on your proposal, contract, or RFP, you then thank your customer and tell them you need to start the process moving so they can receive the goods and services as soon as possible. It is best to have two complete original copies of your proposal, contract, or RFP with all supporting literature such as engineering drawing and reports, or manufacturer specifications. This way both you and your customer will have the identical documents for operations to proceed. Always have electronic and hard original copies of the PO or contracts. I have had incidences when management had a computer failure losing all their records and my personal physical hard copies saved the day.

At one time during my career when I was competing for a large service contract and my competitor had a lower hourly rate. I felt my price was going too high and I attached a comic strip from *Hagar the Viking* of a war party marching through a dark forest trail. The lead scout discovers a broken arrow in the path and says, "I found this broken arrow in the trail, what does it mean?". The commander looks at the broken arrow and replied, "Low bidder got the contract.". The old saying comes to mind, "you get what you pay for". The purpose of attaching this comic to my proposal was to have the customer realize that price is not everything. You can take your family out to dinner at McDonalds and spend $20, or you can dine at Ruth's Chris Steak House and spend $200 - both places will fill your empty tummy, but the difference is in the satisfaction and quality of food along with overall experience.

Other times, RFPs are used by companies looking for long term agreements. They give an outline of the specifications of the service tasks and products they want addressed. The competing bidding companies providing information on how to satisfy those specification of service tasks and products try to present a package that differentiates themselves through their creativity in their presentation package. I took pleasure and pride in selling long term service agreements to commercial and industrial customers. To me, a one-year period is considered short term having the character of too much change and turn over each year, losing consistency. But a multi-year agreement will provide long term consistency of services. If your customer changes their supplier of services annually, the quality of the products and services can suffer due to a lack of consistency. Many times I would capture a new long-term maintenance agreement and find the equipment in sad condition because of the many annual changes in service contractors.

With industrial customers, long term agreements for OEM machinery is very common. The supplying vendor becomes a partner with their customer delivering components that enhance the quality and profitability of their customer's product. These long-term customer agreements, if serviced with quality using good communications, can build strong business relationships with you and the company that you represent. I captured many long-term agreements lasting fifteen to twenty five years. I retained those customers even when ownership changed hands or key personnel retired, transferred, or even passed away. With long term agreements you become part of their business plan, a line item in their budget.

There was a large western region hotel chain that had annual facility meetings which I was invited to regularly as a participant. I traveled to Los Angeles and Phoenix bringing in speakers from our factories who presented the latest industrial information on manufacturing designs and procedures. Having a strong relationship with this customer, I was also invited to play in their annual company golf tournaments. This is the result of building a trusting relationship over time by delivering on our agreements and being there when the customer would rely on your knowledge and experience to assist him in his daily responsibilities.

There is a saying I used many times during my career, "good things take time, just like fine wine.". Being responsive and persistent will eventually pay off. Sometimes slow and steady wins the race, like the childhood story about the race between the tortoise and rabbit teaches. The tortoise won while the rabbit slowed down to brag about his great deeds that were yet to happen.

In preparing your proposals make the best of your time. Gather a team of knowledgeable people if needed and use your creative mind to produce the best proposal you can and chances of being rewarded the contract will increase.

CHAPTER 37

Communicating Wins

Communication with all who are involved with a sale, which may include your project manager, the technicians who do the work, the billing department, the shipping and receiving personnel and your customer's team, can make all the difference in the outcome of your project.

Once you complete you still need to make sure everyone on your team understands what was sold. For example, I once sold a major repair on a large air conditioning compressor to an international cruise liner company. Their ship was in port for its scheduled annual repair and maintenance services. I explained to our lead technician that all communications for anything outside the scope of services needed to be approved by the customer's project manager on the ship by the name of Phil. The repairs and maintenance on the compressor took about three weeks to complete and I kept in touch with our lead technician on the progress of the job during that time who said everything was moving along without any difficulties. After the project was completed, I looked over the invoice and discovered that there were a lot of extra services performed outside the defined scope of the agreement. I asked our lead tech if he had received permission from Phil to perform these extra services. He said a man by the name of Sammy gave him permission on all the extra services, not Phil. I asked him if Phil was aware of Sammy giving permission on the extra services which amounted to over $40K. What ended up happening was my manager and I had to drive up to their North American corporate office in Seattle and explain to their senior operations manager why we sent them an invoice that was $40K more than the agreement amount. My manager and I were in quite a pickle. We had no written authorization on the extra services, and Sammy, who was giving our technician the verbal approval on the extra services was only a subcontractor and not even employed by the cruise liner company.

The operations manager told my manager that there was no way he was going to issue payment for the extra $40K in services that were not authorized by Phil. The cruise liner corporate operations manager finally took pity on our situation and agreed to pay us only half of the true extra amount ($20K). If our lead technician had followed the instructions given and had contacted Phil or even me during the repairs, we would not have lost $20K on the project. Possibly I should have been paying closer attention to the project by visiting the job site and touching base with Phil more often. Our technician had done many projects for this customer over the years, and I felt with all his experience on a job of this caliber things should have gone more smoothly.

Therefore, stay close to your projects even when you have someone else managing them for you. A little bit of communication with your onsite team and with your customer during a project can secure loose ends and maximize your profits.

CHAPTER 38

National Agreements are Good Business

When you can capture a contract sale with multiple sites covering a large geographical region, consider how your products and services can best help your customer. You may have to start out small with one or two sites, but the future growth potentials can be great.

Early in my career I was told never to use the word 'contract'. Contract is a little too strong of a word, too binding and legal sounding. Instead, we were told to use the word agreement, which felt more team-oriented and friendly, a coming together on an understanding of what is to be achieved and accomplished. Just like the word sales. The term 'sale' gives a feeling of trying to force something on another person who may not be convinced on a product or just does not want or need what is being offered. Companies came up with titles for their sales personnel like: Business Development, Account Manager or Marketing Representative. During my career I think I've seen most of these titles used on my business cards. Choosing friendly verbiage when describing yourself and what you do can help in creating a more bonding feeling with those you interact with in the business community.

I was calling on an international hotel chain in downtown Portland, Oregon and was able to secure a large overhaul on their two, twenty-five-year-old large 300 horsepower air conditioning compressors that serviced their twenty-story facility. The main compressor bearings needed to be replaced and were no longer inventoried at the manufacturer. I was able to communicate the importance of replacing the failing bearings to complete the overhaul, making the compressors operational for the coming air conditioning season. My contact at the manufacturer located the pattern at the foundry, had the bearing cased and machined. The cost was $9K for the new bearings. The customer approved the extra cost, and we completed the repair in time for the air conditioning season.

I believe long term maintenance agreements are best for critical pieces of equipment, and once the overhaul of the two machines were completed I discussed the advantages of a long-term preventive maintenance agreement with the facility manager. For some reason he did not believe in maintenance agreements. Every year he would bid out the annual services for the two air conditioning compressors and every year a different low bidding contractor would be awarded the annual services.

During our company's annual western regional meeting a salesperson from Los Angeles stated that our company had entered into a national agreement with that international hotel corporation. When I returned from the regional meeting, I phoned the corporate hotel operations manager contact in Los Angeles who initiated the national agreement and told him about the overhauls on the two compressors at their Portland site and how the facility manager did not believe in maintenance agreements. The operations manager told me he was planning a visit to Portland and that both he and I would meet with his Portland facility manager and have him approve our maintenance program.

The date and time were set when the regional operations manager would arrive in Portland, and we agreed to meet with his facility manager at their downtown hotel. We greeted the facility manager in the hotel lobby that morning and went to his office to discuss the two air conditioning compressors. I felt a real sense of power when the regional operations manager told the Portland facility manager that he was to purchase a multi-year maintenance program from me with his approved maintenance specifications. If it had not been for that national agreement, I would have probably never been able to close any kind of program with that facility manager.

When you are out in the marketplace representing your company trying to sell goods and services, it never hurts to ask about how large their operation is because then you can present them with the option of a national agreement covering all their sites. Utilizing the internet, you can access information on their locations. If you are meeting with a purchasing agent, you can always introduce the idea of a blanket PO or national agreement that can cover all their locations. Of course, the company you are selling for must have the resources and ability to provide those services on a regional or national level.

We had a local hotel chain based in my sales territory and were doing some services for them, but only in our local area. One day, while calling on one of their local hotels, the facility manager said I should speak with his supervisor at their local corporate office and gave me the person's name and phone number. I called, introduced myself, and set up an appointment. That first meeting was the beginning of a long relationship that lasted many years, and we are still good friends to this day. As time passed, we started doing more and more business. We reached a point where I was able to present a national agreement for all fifty-seven of their hotels located throughout the western United States. During that time there were many large purchases for new equipment. Also, I enjoyed the social and economic rewards. Always keep the big picture in mind while developing your customer relationships, and the possibilities of national/regional agreements. You will constantly need to deliver on those agreements. Stay close to your customers to ensure that your company is providing all the requirements of those agreements. A good national agreement customer may give you a couple chances to redeem yourself when failures occur before looking for another vendor.

CHAPTER 39

There is Always an Exception to the Rule

Rules are made, laws are passed and in history we see the rules change with the times as technologies and cultures adapt to those changes by ways of persuasion and economic powers. When buyers purchase at a higher price for an equal product or service, they seem to be going against the idea of trying to save money for their company. They make an exception, thinking they will be better off in the long run. When a manager hires a person who has no experience for a critical position, they are taking an exception and risk thinking things will work out for the best.

When I was hired by Carrier Corporation to grow their aftermarket services, one of the main requirements for that position was a college degree. Fortunately, I had attended Washington State University and received a Bachelor of Arts in English Literature with a Minor in Business Management. Throughout my career there was always someone giving me advice on how to sell. I concluded that everyone seems to be an expert on how to sell and were willing to offer their opinions and advice. I would listen to their suggestions and points of view, then utilize what I thought would best help me succeed in closing more sales. I was always the one out in front of the customers trying to close business and all those advisors were still in support positions back in the office. We are all in it together. How we present ourselves to the customer is a reflection on everyone in the company you are representing, creating your reputation in the marketplace.

A friend of mine who operated a large dealership service company for an air conditioning manufacturer once told me he would only hire college educated salespeople because he felt they were more polished. He himself has an Electrical Engineering degree. People who have college degrees like to hire people like themselves who have had some of the same experiences.

During my career I have seen several exceptions to this college educated rule for hiring managers and salespeople. The culture of upper management is largely made up of college educated people, many with masters and doctoral degrees. I have a friend who broke through this college degree ceiling of the upper levels of the corporate world. He only had a high school degree and a journeyman level electrician's license. While growing up, his father was working as an electrical contractor for a small hotel chain with only a few locations. Years passed and the hotel chain grew to over fifty locations. His father by then was a major employee of that hotel chain and was able to hire his son into the maintenance department. When I met his son years later he was the Corporate Facility Manager for all their sites, working closely with the CEO on matters of managing the business. I was able to close a large national agreement with him along with selling them many large air conditioning units. Later the hotel chain sold and he moved on to a new company becoming Vice President of Operations, managing over 1,200 facilities across North America. As of today, he is the Facility Operations Manager for a large natural gas utility company.

As you move through your selling career try to keep in touch with those people you've developed good relationships with because you never know what positions of power they may come to occupy.

The air conditioning company I was employed with started promoting technicians into management and sales positions. There was one technician in Seattle, Washington that was promoted into a sales position and was very successful. By using his technical background and his relationships in the marketplace he went on to become one of the top salespersons in the Seattle market. He presented himself professionally and achieved a prominent level of selling, securing many major accounts.

That old friend of mine who owned the HVAC service company ended up selling the company to one of his technicians. When that technician first started working for that company, he was smart enough to let my owner friend know that he wanted to learn as much as possible about the business so in the future he might be able to run the company. Over the years the owner trained that technician in all the operational sectors of the company. Today that one technician is now the owner of that multi-million-dollar air conditioning company. The company is now one of the largest HVAC dealership service companies in the area.

Some people will never go beyond their station in life while others move to higher levels. There is nothing wrong with that, it is just how things sometimes happen. Most of the population are good, hard working people just trying to get through their lives the best they can. From the person who picks up your garbage to the CEO, I like to believe we are all just doing the best we can - caring for our loved ones.

There will always be occurrences during your career when exceptions will be made, and hopefully those outcomes will be positive.

CHAPTER 40

The Little Things Can Matter

It is surprising how the little details can make a difference in how you present yourself during your business day. What you say, how body language is perceived, or how detailed your proposals are, sometimes determine whether you win or lose a sale.

I was always excited about meeting that first contact, that person behind the door, that new potential customer. Not knowing what that person would be like, their personality, their history excited me. How would I present myself and my goods and services? As I entered and approached my new prospect, I would try to have a friendly smile and handshake. Sometimes the person would squeeze my hand hard and I would return the gesture. If they just grab the ends of fingers on your hand and squeeze them hard, that reflects that the person wants to show themselves as an authority, someone who may think of themselves as being in charge. The saying goes that people judge one another in the first ten to thirty seconds. The main thing is, you are in front of a potential buyer and this is an opportunity to present yourself and the products to someone who may purchase them. You are both sizing each other up by conversing on topics of interest: weather, sports, hometowns, traffic, little talk to relax the atmosphere prior to presenting your true purpose in being there. As I have stated previously, limit your turn talking to no more than three minutes or you will start to come across as hogging the conversation. Try to let your customers be the leader in the conversation. Remember, people usually like to talk about themselves, but you will need to adjust to different personalities. You are also trying to determine if this person can issue contracts or expedite orders.

When you exchange business cards and you discover that the person you are meeting with has a title of Purchasing Agent, President or CFO, then you are speaking with the right person. I try to keep the conversation calm and with comfortable topics. Conversation is one of the main building blocks to creating a relationship. Sometimes I start by commenting on my drive to their location, the scenery, road conditions, the security clearance of their company, their latest safety training I attended, how friendly and helpful the receptionist was, a business article I had read about their industry, or the news about a new company moving into the area. All these topics can put the first meetings into a comfortable state. Once the conversational exchange begins, always give your prospect plenty of time to respond and do not interrupt the person while they are speaking. You may notice something in their office of interest such as a picture or award, a mounted fish, hunting trophy or souvenir. Let the person tell their story about the item. In making the person feel important by having them talk more about themselves you will become educated about them. Once I walked into a person's office and there was a giant marlin mounted on the wall. Obviously the person was a fisherman - fish stories are always a good topic.

I always thank the person for taking time to meet with me. If I thought my day was busy, their day was most likely busier. Time is precious. Time is money. Use time cautiously and as wisely as possible but also try to enjoy it. Time is best enjoyed during the business day when the customer sees a sincere smile and an upbeat, positive attitude. Then they will be more likely to engage in friendly conversation. Sometimes this friendly exchange will only occur for a few minutes or less and other times when your relationship is more developed, personal conversation can last longer until it is time for business to be discussed.

Starting questions like "how's your day going?" may sound simple, but the way your customer responds will give you a feel on how to proceed in the conversation. Being empathetic and understanding is an effective way to connect.

Be aware of your surroundings, they can give you a lot of information on the state of your customer's business. For example, if the parking lot is filled, their business could be booming. If the parking lot is almost empty with only a few cars and there is a demolition crane on site, the business atmosphere might be bleak. The old saying "keep your ears and eyes open" is always applicable when calling on customers throughout your day.

Those little things are signs that can help direct you on to the correct path, giving you that extra bit of information that will help you understand and win a new customer, capture that big contract, or build strong relationships.

CHAPTER 41

Good Relationships Build Strong Business

When there is a strong connection between a salesperson and a customer, a relationship-type of respect will exist. Good business relationships take time to develop, and every transaction can strengthen those relationships.

One of the main reasons I started writing about my life in sales is that I am concerned about the ongoing developments of the internet and technology causing a decline in personal interactions. That person-to-person selling, that interaction, might be decreasing bringing about a decline in the ability to read and understand body language. The other day I was on the phone with a friend of mine on the east coast who has been a sales manager for several years and has been recently promoted to President running a well-known HVAC mechanical contracting company. I asked him if he has seen a decline in his personal interactions with his customers due to the internet. He told me that business is generated by relationships, that business is, in fact, all about relationships. This, of course, is what I was hoping he would say and what I strongly believe as well.

A few years ago I was making my scheduled sales call on a county facility department in southern Oregon. To get to their office you had to take an elevator in the courthouse to the fourth floor and then walk four flights of stairs to their office at the top of the building. I would appear every three months with an appointment in advance to visit with their facilities manager to discuss the status of our maintenance agreements covering their air conditioning equipment. During a conversation on one of my visits the manager told me that a personal visit was a rare occurrence since not many salespeople ever took the time to visit them in their office. I enjoyed meeting those people in that rooftop office, and I was able to build a good working relationship with them over the years.

During a luncheon conversation one day with a family friend of mine who works in the private banking industry, I asked him about how he goes about keeping and growing his clientele. He told me that he has never solicited any of his customers and said that almost all his old and new clients were through word of mouth, referrals from his existing clients and social friends. He said that his business is completely based on person-to-person interaction which grew into a network of business relationships.

Of course, to build a good business relationship you first need the opportunity to prove yourself as a dependable person who can deliver the products and services you represent. Your actions on delivering on your comments to your customers is what selling is all about, so care for them, give them something extra that will strengthen the business, the friendship. Regularly keep in touch with customers and your business will prosper. Take care of those who take care of you!

During my last employment we had a large office team meeting on diversity. During the meeting I made the comment that what people like is to be respected - respect for what they do on a day-to-day basis. All of us are trying to do the best we can in this life providing for our loved ones and just dealing with all the unexpected things that can happen, trying to accomplish what is required to maintain a happy and secure life. I believe if you give respect you will have a better chance of receiving respect. If you can build a respectable rapport with those you encounter, sometimes they will tell you their story, revealing something personal about themselves which may bring the possibility of beginning a strong relationship.

Once I was selling my products to the ship repair companies and developed a good friendship with one of the buyers. I was in my mid-thirties at the time and my customer friend was in his mid-fifties. We had played golf together at annual vendor tournaments and met for drinks and lunch many times. One day we were having lunch at a local restaurant when he told me a very personal thing that he was dealing with. Since I had known him he had always had a very deep, gravelly-sounding voice. What he told me was that in the past he had throat cancer and that it had returned. I was taken aback by what he was sharing with me. He then said he had decided not to go with the doctor's recommendation for radiation treatment. He said the treatment was just too miserable and not worth it. That was the last time I saw him. Six weeks later he passed away. I never forgot him. He was a good person, respected by his fellow employees and his many friends. When a customer opens up and reveals personal things about themselves, it is a special thing. This happens when the time and place are right and when the relationship has developed a high level of trust. When the relationship is such that you feel you can trust each other, revealing personal aspects will surface.

Being sincere and personal with your customers can create trust and loyalty that may last several years. Having good relationships can be very rewarding on a personal level and may develop monetary rewards.

CHAPTER 42

Stay Close to Your Team

A long time ago someone gave me some words of advice: "Take care of those who take care of you". It is a simple statement with a very strong message. When you are in the middle of a large project that incorporates many players, you need to have everyone aware of all aspects of that project as it moves along to its completion. Try to be understanding, appreciative and sympathetic to your teammates. The closer you stay to your team during a project or business transaction the better the outcome.

During conversations with my business peers, we eventually end up discussing those situations where we had to internally sell what was going to be sold; meaning that we had a wonderful opportunity to close a sale and we were confident that it would be profitable, but we still had to convince the branch manager, regional manager, technicians or project managers that the sale was truly a good and profitable venture. After long negotiations and some concessions your team comes to an agreement and the sale is finally internally agreed upon. The salesperson wants to close the sale at a competitive price while it seems management and operations only want to avoid all possible risk while maximizing profit.

I was working with a project manager once who believed in applying an extra 10% to my final pricing to cover any unforeseen occurrences or contingencies. If you note in your proposal that anything outside the described scope of work will be addressed separately, the customer is then aware that those unforeseen items will be priced and invoiced separately. Therefore, the need to add the extra 10% should be unnecessary. Putting an extra 10% on your proposal pricing will make you less competitive and decrease your chance of closing the sale.

When I was with Carrier Corporation selling service agreements and air conditioning projects, I also developed business in the southern half of the state to a point where it justified locating a full-time technician to that area. We needed about $200K per year in business to financially cover the cost of a technician to relocate there. At the time we were doing around $400K per year in this region. Having a technician in the southern region would make us more price-competitive by decreasing travel and lodging expenses which represented thousands of dollars. I presented this to the branch manager explaining if we did not act on this our competitors would, and we would lose our existing customers in that area. The branch manager told me that I would need to present a complete study to justify moving a technician to that region. I couldn't believe what I was hearing! There was more than enough evidence to justify this business decision. A good manager would move a technician into that area in a heartbeat and reap the business rewards. I concluded that this service manager did not want the extra responsibility and did not have the business savvy to handle the growth in business.

During my 24 years with Carrier I witnessed seven branch service managers come and go. To me it seemed that the corporation was unwilling to provide the necessary support to make the branch or any branch for that matter prosper. In some cases, they would hire an unexperienced and unqualified person to manage the branch, other times they would hire a good manager who they wouldn't give the tools needed to grow the business. The sarcastic corporation moto among the sales team became "do more with less" and what everyone finds out is that you cannot do more with less! Upper management would want their managers to grow their business by increasing sales. When the manager would request funds to hire a new salesperson they would say we first needed to increase our sales. It becomes a catch 22 situation. How can you increase sales without increasing your sales team? It seemed that corporate management wants to have their cake and eat it too. Accounting and finance people only see the numbers and if the numbers don't support an additional sales position, then you are out of luck.

Not only does a salesperson have to sell their pricing on projects and adapt to the changing market, they also need to be selling to their support teams because after the process of closing a sale, the operations side takes responsibility for executing major parts that make up the sale to its completion. Correct components need to be purchased and delivered to the job site on time to meet the agreed completion schedules of the projects. Labor needs to be assigned and scheduled to meet the proposed requirements. Invoicing needs to be performed correctly and in a timely matter, possibly partial or progress billing may be required for larger projects that need upfront material purchases and long-term labor expenditures. A salesperson needs to support and work closely with his operations team. Praising your team builds their confidence. When something goes sideways like a late delivery of a crucial component, a sudden change of scheduling or a miscalculated invoice, communications with your team and your customer is critical. The sooner a problem is addressed and resolved the better it is for all parties. Then you can move on, addressing the closure of new business opportunities. I always make sure I thank those who work with me on all my projects, letting them know I appreciate their efforts and how the customer is feeling throughout the project to its completion. When your team is aware of the customer's feelings and opinions on how the job is progressing, they will become more bonded, striving for a high satisfaction level for the customer. During the business day your team is communicating with your customers for scheduling, deliveries of components and project information. So *take care of those who care for you.* If everyone is on the same page of satisfying the customer and are aware of how the customer is feeling, things will have a better chance of moving along smoothly to the project's completion. Communication is an important key to having a successful project or transaction with a customer. The company you sell for is only as good as how your customer perceives you.

The last company I was employed with promoted a person with poor selling skills. He had changed employers seven times in a five-year period but was promoted to the position of sales manager. The manager who promoted him also had no selling experience. Right off, this new sales manager wanted to know what our strategies would be to reach our end of the year goals, so he composed a page and a half questionnaire on the topic. It seemed very strange that he and his manager wanted to know what our detailed strategies were on attaining our goals. I felt that I was hired because I already knew how to do my job and there should be no need to explain it. It was as if this new sales manager did not know how to sell so we were supposed to teach him. One of the questions he asked that reflected his inability to understand sales was, "what would you do differently this year with your telephone conversations with customers to meet your sales goals?". First, I believe every conversation is unique and how you interact with customers on the phone depends on personalities, subject matter and issues involved. The ability to think on your feet and your conversation savvy come into play; what is the purpose of the phone call? Obviously, this new sales manager did not have those qualities. I have seen this more than once when management places a poorly performing salesperson into a sales management position. This unqualified sales manager probably spent most of his time in the office kissing up to their superiors instead of outside the office in the marketplace selling where the real action is.

One time our marketing department wanted to perform a customer survey on their response to a cover letter attached to the rebate payment checks. The survey consisted of two pages of questions. This new sales manager volunteered the sales team to execute the survey. Of course, I was not happy about bothering my customers during their busy day to answer multiple questions on some survey that I felt was a waste of time for the both of us. I felt the survey should not be a function of the sales team. The marketing department created the survey; therefore, they should be the ones responsible for it. So I asked the marketing department if they could telephone my customers and perform the survey for me since they were the ones who created the survey. They said they were just too busy, as if the salespeople were not! We were just trying to reach our sales goals and find new customers so the department could reach its goals. This new sales manager did not have the backbone to tell the marketing department to do the survey themselves.

Later that week I was talking with a good friend of mine in a different sales department and he gave me a great idea - just fill out the surveys yourself! No one will ever know, your customers will not be bothered, and I can make myself look like I am doing a wonderful job with the customers. The marketing department ended up happy because they got what they wanted and when it was all over, everyone was happy. I was the only salesperson to hand in my dozen completed surveys. Just think of all the meetings with all the marketing personnel and all the hours wasted it took to create a survey that was unwarranted. One person could have created the survey, contacted the customers and reported all pertinent findings. The odd thing was the marketing department did not even consider including the sales team in what type of questions and information might help us in doing our job. So the next time someone asks you to perform a task that is outside your position of sales and that takes you away from accomplishing your mission to expand business, just nod your head and say you will do the best you can. Then be creative, save as much time as possible on the task or just put it away on the back burner and keep doing what you were hired to do: sell. If you find yourself in hot water over some required task you were not hired to do, just be very apologetic, sing the blues of how you were just too busy dealing with closing sales and managing customer needs.

Customers occasionally will place a date and time when the order will be issued. We don't have time to stall the process waiting on our superiors for their input and cannot wait, so we move ahead and deliver the proposal. Cases such as these, it is better to ask for forgiveness than permission. Management put you in a position where you had to respond to your customer. The company can always turn the order down or reject the contract terms, but you did what you are paid to do: make sales!

Take care of those who take care of you and stay close to your teammates. This will give you that extra element in completing a profitable sale and create a happy customer who will call you when they are in a time of need.

Know Your Assigned Goals

You need to be aware of your personal goals along with your assigned company goals, so you plan a road map of your business and financial future. Once you know what your personal financial goals are, you then start setting up business customer targets so you can achieve those company goals.

Are you achieving your goals? Once a year salespeople get their sales numbers they need to achieve for the coming year. Companies love to forecast and the only way they can plan for the company's future is by giving goals to their sales departments to achieve. Numbers come down from an owner or a CEO and his team of upper corporate managers who are trying to meet the demands of the board of directors who are constantly driven by the demands of Wall Street. What I learned over the years is that if you constantly focus on those corporate sales goals, you get too caught up in trying to reach those goal numbers and end up getting stressed out and lose sight of how to do your job in a professional manner. When I receive my sales goals for the new year, I put them in my desk drawer or file them away someplace in my computer and try not to look at them again. If you work hard and do the best you can, usually the chips will fall in your favor. Sometimes the sales goals you achieve are fair and realistic, and other times they are not. If a company wants to eliminate a poorly performing salesperson or just wants to get rid of a salesperson, all they need to do is give him sales goals that are unattainable and totally unrealistic. It happened to me, even when I had developed a very strong a profitable customer base over many years. Bringing in good, profitable business even during the economic recession of 2008-2009.

During that last recession Carrier Corporation probably looked at my 401K balance, my pension benefits, incentive payouts and salary and felt they could increase their profits by replacing me with a younger person whom they could pay much less and without a pension program. They said I should be selling at a much higher level (remember this was 2009 when unemployment was almost 8%). Companies were laying off people and going out of business. The regional manager presented me with a performance plan that there was no way I could achieve. I knew what this regional manager was doing and requested that I wanted to take the performance plan home that evening and look it over with my wife and sign it the next day. He told me, "You sign it now, or you walk.". So, I signed it knowing that my days were numbered. With my signature that document became a legal agreement. Having signed their performance plan the corporation would be off the hook for any legal actions I could bring. But after much thought and discussion with friends I concluded that I really didn't want to be employed by a company that treats one of their top performers so poorly. Then I thought about all the long-term stress and financial burden of a lengthy legal battle, and I declined to pursue that direction. Carrier had almost unlimited legal funds for fighting such cases. I had only my retirement savings. The lawyers would be the only winners. Four months later when I arrived at my office to start my work week, I was given a cardboard box to collect my personal belongings and then I was driven home by a fellow employee. After twenty-four years of making a tremendous amount of revenues and profits for this company, I was shown the door without any severance. The lesson here is to be aware of your surroundings and the personnel changes within your company who have authority to harm you. Remember to save money and have funds available in case you have a sudden change in your employment environment.

CHAPTER 44

Understanding Your Boss

Understanding what your manager is responsible for will help build a good working environment between you. Your manager has demands and business goals set upon them, and only their operations team and salespeople can help them attain those goals.

During my lengthy career in the selling profession, I have had many managers, supervisors, bosses and overseers seemingly to always want greater sales numbers from my efforts. Some of these managers have not been so desirable, lacking in management skills and a few had no experience at all. The ones I liked best were the remote managers who visited occasionally to see how I went about my business day. I had a close business friend who once made the statement, "let people do what they do". Meaning don't stand in the way of whatever a person is best at. Utilize their expertise. Learn from the engineer, learn from the pipe fitter, the rigging contractor, the shipping clerk. Give them respect and they will respond with better communications and perform at a higher level. Don't clog them down with multiple reports. Positive energy usually responds positively. When your manager is requesting more sales growth, agree with them!

Growth in sales is growth in the business and more money for everyone. Why wouldn't you want more growth? If you are incentivized on the commissions of your sales, then of course you want to make as much money as possible. Therefore, you and your boss will both be on the same page, wanting to be as successful as possible.

I have heard stories about sales managers who wanted to know almost everything the salesperson was doing, down to every last phone call, appointment, discussion, when, what and why. This type of reporting takes massive amounts of time away from what the salesperson is supposed to be doing: selling! The time spent reporting all this information causes the salesperson want to just make some of it up so they have enough time to do the job they were hired to do. I have seen salespeople get so caught up in doing reports that their numbers start to decline to the point that the stability of their employment becomes questionable.

This type of manager who demands reporting all your activities is hurting not only you but also the company. A good sales manager lets his team function independently, assisting them with questions that arise such as pricing, terms and conditions, having discussions on strategies concerning difficult customers and keeping them well informed about what is happening in their market so they can adjust their strategies accordingly and inform them on the latest developments in products and technologies, scheduled trade shows and conferences in order to socialize with customers and competitors in their industry, giving them that professional edge when they are out in their market.

I had a supervisor once who was based in San Francisco and we would meet every few months to discuss the status of sales and spend the day calling on customers. We would also have telephone conversations every so often if something came up that I thought I should run by him for his opinion. He gave me some advice which I am sure he gave to all the sales team. He told me one day to approach sales as if it were my own business. Basically, he was telling me to take ownership of my efforts in the marketplace. When your customers see how personally involved you are with their purchases and projects your business relationship will become stronger and you will start to become part of your customer's company. Prior to becoming the Regional Sales Manager, my supervisor was a top sales performer. He knew how to relate when one of his salesmen had a difficult customer and was able to give credible advice based on his own experiences.

In the sales profession you are always required to do some type of reporting on your activities. It is only normal. Companies like to know what you are working on and what you have sold for forecasting purposes so they can report those findings on up the corporate ladder of power. The funny thing is, a sales report sounds more like what is already sold and almost always the company already has good records of what is sold and amounts of revenue that was generated by an individual salesperson. I always kept a record of my sales calls on my calendar and would keep a separate folder for individual customers. That gave me the ability to look back and see what and how much each customer was generating. This would help me see who I should be contacting, what items need following up on, and who I need to touch base with to see what's going on with any item with interest with that customer. Are they still open for business? What new persons do I need to be making connections with? Is it time for them to purchase again?

A family friend of mine who sells fleets of semi-trucks in the global market had just returned from Saudi Arabia when the CEO entered his office and wanted to know how the sales trip went. My friend first presented the required corporate sales report from his meetings with the Saudi government personnel. The CEO was satisfied with the report, but then my friend handed over his personal notes on the meetings. I am sure the CEO was very pleased with the extra personal notes from the meeting that went beyond what was required.

Having been in countless meetings with customers I always try to have a tablet, folder, or journal booklet to record the meeting. Who was in attendance? What was the topic of the meeting? What decisions were made? What course of actions were decided on? Who is going to what and when? What problems were addressed and how were they resolved? By taking notes during meetings with customers they will see that you value their time and shows them that you understand the meeting's importance. Keeping a record of the meeting in a folder or laptop file can become valuable when people start forgetting decisions or statements that were made. When appropriate, you can follow up with a summary of a meeting in written form, addressed to all attendees to bring everyone together and prevent any misunderstandings.

I don't recommend taking your laptop to meetings for recording purposes. It is too impersonal and places a physical barrier between you and your customer or your audience. They cannot see what you are writing or doing on the backside of the screen. Laptops ca be great for visual presentations, showing what a product looks like, how it operates, diagrams, drawings, or testimonials. PowerPoint presentations can be dangerous though as they can become impersonal. You should be doing the selling, not your computer. Remember, you are the one doing the selling not some corporate marketing video. Buyers are people and like to relate and do business with real people.

While selling HVAC multi-year service programs, on several occasions I would set up my laptop and the customer would critique the service agreement to their liking. Once we were satisfied with the changes, I would email the agreement of services to them right then and there, print out two copies in their office (one for me and one for the customer) so they could sign the agreement and I would depart with a signature to proceed with the agreed upon program.

I kept electronic files and hard copies of all my signed contracts and purchase orders from all my customers. When it came time for a sales report, I would have all my sales organized by date, so all I had to do was to query a particular time period and all my orders would appear for that week, month or quarter, saving a tremendous amount of time and allowing myself more time to concentrate on closing new business. The lesson here is to create your own system of recording that will save you time, simplifying the reporting process. Time is money and being efficient is the key to increasing business and income.

CHAPTER 45

Be Nice to Management

Doctor Peter believed that in organizations people are promoted beyond their level of competence into a state of incompetence. I think we all have experienced this during our careers. An example would be the person who approved the O-ring seal on the Discovery Space Shuttle that failed. That disaster cost the lives of astronauts and set back the Space Shuttle program for years. We had a president of the company who was highly educated with a Master of Business Administration from Harvard Business School and was a West Point graduate. He was very hard working and intellectually brilliant. He hired an Army Captain Ranger with a Civil Engineering degree who was leaving the military for the private business sector. After six months of training in the marketplace he was quickly promoted as Service Manager to our local branch. The only thing this person had ever been exposed to was the military life. He thought in terms of chain of command and only listened to his superiors or upper management for advice and seemed to never listen to his team members or those with years of experience. Orders were given, followed out and your commanding officer was never questioned. Being in the military, he had never been exposed to a profit/ loss business environment. In the military it was just spend and spend. I remember one conversation we had were he requested me to do something that made no sense whatsoever and would have damaged a business relationship and cost the company a large sum of money. I told him no. He just stood there dumbfounded. I believe it was the first time someone outside his military experience verbally told him no. He could not grasp that a subordinate would flat out refuse his request. It was a situation where he was hired by the president of the company and put on the fast track for an upper management position, so it really didn't matter how well he performed his job.

For example, when he first started, I was the only salesperson and had to give him 50% of my accounts to manage. After three months as a salesperson, he was promoted to Branch Manager and kept all those accounts while performing the tasks of Service Manager. After he had managed those accounts for a couple of years, only one remained. That means out of the thirty-five active accounts he started with, only one remained. After that he was promoted to National Sales Manager.

Dr. Peter is probably smiling from above right now. This person was one of those people who believe if they are given a title that it will automatically bring with it all the respect, knowledge, and experience to perform that position. My advice is don't be like this. It is best to listen to those around you who have knowledge and experience. Ask questions if you are not sure about something. Listen to your teammates. Learn by building rapport and confidence with one another. If you have one of those managers who doesn't listen to their team, just keep selling, caring for your customer, and communicate your concerns and needs as honestly as you can and hopefully things will work out for the best. Remember, positive energy produces positive energy. If things don't work out for the best, start considering other more positive alternatives.

Help your manager compile data for their supervisor so they can plan appropriately for the future. Sometimes it is difficult to provide your manager with what they want or think they want. In the long run it is better to do the best you can and keep them happy. A happy manager is a good manager and more enjoyable to work with.

CHAPTER 46

Happy Workers Are Productive Workers

Happy workers are productive workers. This may sound a little silly, but I've heard it since I started working on the farm as a kid and I believe it still holds true today. Organizational behavioral studies have shown over and over that the happier the work environment the higher the productivity level. The question is how to create happy workers! Do you give longer vacations, parental leave, pizza Fridays, company outings, strong 401Ks, good health care programs, Thursday morning massage.....?

When people feel good about themselves and what they do for a living the emotional drama that gets in the way of accomplishing goals decreases. In a business environment if the people who produce the goods and services (from upper management to front-line personnel) work together as a cohesive team, quality and productivity will increase.

I know of a young energy engineering company who started their business only seven years ago with two people and now employ close to forty employees and have the reputation of being one of the top energy engineering firms. At their office location you will see a full-size shuffleboard, dart board, pool table, a café setting with micro beers on tap, everyone is dressed casually, and during Thursday lunch hour they have a private physical trainer come to lead workouts for whoever wishes to attend. They also have an excellent healthcare plan, 401Ks with financial planners, and a free lunch on Fridays! When you enter their office you feel more like you entered an old-time café brew pub. Applicants are constantly trying to get employed there and are even willing to take pay cuts to get hired. The owner created a new relaxed office environment where employees can work productively at their own rate, resulting in a higher quality product. Recently the company (for its size) was awarded the top company to work for in the State!

I knew of an industrial hose and fitting company in Spokane, Washington where all the employees were on a salary plus a commission profit sharing program. The company is the largest hose and fitting business in eastern Washington and northern Idaho. The employees feel they were part of the big picture focusing on the future of the company. They felt they had ownership in what they do for a living. If the company is doing good, they would be rewarded with higher incomes giving them the incentive to provide services to their customers at a higher level.

If you have an unhappy employee that interacts with customers, that poor attitude will cause them to take their business elsewhere where they will be treated kindly and with respect. I had a service agreement with a hospital, providing preventive maintenance on their HVAC system. The hospital had a security program that required all visiting contractors to have clearance prior to performing any services and they must wear an access badge from the security department. Our lead technician was scheduled to perform maintenance on their main air conditioning compressor. His arrogance made him feel that he did not need to check in with the hospital's security and went straight to the location of the air conditioning unit that needed servicing. A security guard for the hospital confronted our technician about not having an access clearance badge and restricted him from proceeding with his services. Our technician was not happy with the confrontation, and while departing he called the hospital security officer a foul name. The next morning I received a phone call from the facility manager telling me what happened. Of course, I replied that this is not how we treat our customers and I would take care of the issue, promising him the technician would be reprimanded and disciplined. I met with my branch service manager who only gave the technician two days off without pay for his actions. Unhappy employees with poor attitudes can cause unpleasant occurrences and customers will lose confidence with your company and start looking at your competition so they will be serviced and treated properly.

If you make employees feel like they are part of the bigger picture, as an important team member of the company, they will perform at a professionally higher level. I had a couple of very successful years selling for Carrier Corporation. At the time, our company president was a good, experienced man and he issued me stock options with the parent company. I felt I was more than just another employee but more as an owner in the company. From then on, I addressed my customers from the viewpoint as a company owner, not just a hired worker. When you personally feel part of a company, your performance and attitude towards your teammates and customers is much more positive.

The higher-level corporate salespeople are treated much differently. Expense accounts, company cars, memberships in country clubs, paid vacations, memberships in associations, access to company aircraft, large salaries, bonuses, commissions, and company stocks are incentives to secure the higher performing sales professionals.

"What goes around, comes around" is a saying stated quite often in the business world. If you treat people poorly, it's likely that poor treatment someday will be acted upon you. But if you treat people kindly with good intentions then your life has a better chance of being enjoyable with pleasant outcomes. A good attitude will produce good feelings and a friendlier environment. As I have mentioned in the past, positive energy produces positive outcomes. Turn lemons into lemonade, the saying goes. It is hard to be positive when you feel cornered with no way out and things just aren't working out the way you wanted. But, as George Harrison once said, "all things must pass". The one thing that never changes is that there is always change. Things happen, and out of the blue you get a phone call from a customer looking for your products and services, or a visit with a new customer who has a need that you can satisfy.

There are always peaks and valleys in our lives, but if you keep a positive attitude those valleys will not seem so deep, and those peaks will feel higher. When you have that extra positive "can-do" attitude, you will enjoy your job more and see your sales grow.

CHAPTER 47

Be Friendly With Placement Companies

Whether you like them or not, placement companies are an important part of filling sales and management positions in the business community. Whenever I was contacted or introduced to a placement company, I always presented myself as sincere and professional as possible because you never know when your employment status may change. Companies are bought and sold and new management changes regularly. During my time with Carrier Corporation, I witnessed many upper managers and branch service managers come and go. Placement companies keep a close ear to what is happening with their clients. They have agreements with companies for utilizing their inventory of applicants for hire whom they have prescreened for the qualities required for management and sales positions.

There was a placement company that specialized in the HVAC industry that contacted me for management and selling positions with one of our competitors. At the time I was very unhappy with the management and was researching my options for new employment. The placement company set up a meeting with that competitor, but their offer did not meet my requirements and I stayed with Carrier. There would have been a decrease in benefits, such as loss of vacation time and a poor 401K program. It is best not to make an emotional decision. Sleep on it and visit a decision in the morning with a rested mind that can think it through clearly without all the surrounding noise. Don't give up a secure situation for an unsure situation. When being interviewed by a company that wants you but offers a smaller salary but they say you will make the difference up by the large commissions you will be making is still a 'maybe'. Why would you give up a good salary, weeks of paid vacation and a strong existing customer base and start all over again to achieve what you already have? Calculate the risks and if changing employment or venturing into a new business is worth the move, then move. Decisions in changing employment can be very risky when you are responsible for loved ones and putting your business relationships and reputation on the line.

If you find yourself in a situation where your company wants to take away all your good accounts and customers or changes the incentive commission program to a point where your income greatly decreases, then it might be time to look for greener pastures. This is the time when having a relationship with a placement company will be to your advantage. When there was a drastic change in the incentive program at Carrier and the sales force was going to lose up to 35% in income commissions, almost 90% of the sales team across the country departed for new employment. I am sure that a good portion of those who found new employment benefitted by having a relationship with a placement agency.

When I was a young single man trying to make my way into a better employment situation, I was introduced to a person who worked for a placement agency. Six months later she contacted me about a job that she was trying to fill. An interview appointment was set up with the owner of the company trying to fill an inside sales operations position. I was offered the job, which I accepted. It was a small start up company, and it was there that I was first exposed to selling in the business community.

Sometimes placement companies are called "headhunters" which seems to be a little rough and unfair. Regardless of their nicknames, they play an important part in the business community by filling positions with professional personnel. I ended up having a good relationship with a placement agency to the point of becoming friends with the owner. We would exchange information about management changes in the HVAC industry. The placement company always knew more about what was happening in the industry because he was in close contact with some of the major players not only in my company but also our competitors. The information he passed on to me gave me a better understanding of how and why personnel changes occurred.

When it comes to placement companies, it is best to listen to their offers and information. You never know what the future holds and when and if the time comes that you need help finding new employment, they may offer you a better and quicker connection to greener pastures.

CHAPTER 48

Control Your Stress and Emotions

Being capable of controlling one's emotions can be difficult. Over the years my wife has always told me to have a night of sleep before making decisions and when the morning arrives, my mind will not be cluttered with all the emotions of the day before. Better decisions are made when you are calmer and less stressed.

Throughout my career I had many stressful times dealing with internal personnel who did not see the importance of caring for customers as much as I did. Internal operations would place unnecessary requirements on the sales such as extra forms, reports and procedures that would complicate the sales process. Operations sometimes would require credit reports from customers to determine their financial ability to make payments. Many successful salespeople have told me they have more problems selling internally to their own companies than selling to their customers. I have spent substantial amounts of time in meetings with management concerning pricing, payment schedules, vendor selection and special customer requests to finalize a proposal.

As previously stated, I had problems with a new project manager who believed that once the pricing was completed with all the costs and profit calculations that an extra 10% needed to be added to the price to cover contingencies. What contingencies? I felt this extra 10% was unnecessary because if anything that occurred outside the defined scope of the proposal happened, it could be discussed with the customer and addressed as an extra cost item. Sometimes I would hide a 10% decrease into my pricing knowing that there would be the 10% contingency added later during the pricing review and I would end up with the price I originally felt had the best chance of capturing the sell. As an option we could make the 10% add on contingency a part of the proposal and refund it back to the customer (or say nothing and capture an extra 10% on the project if by chance the sales even happened). We could not add a contingency at all and manage the project so we would increase our profits through efficiencies and working smarter. All these meetings on pricing are basically about minimizing risk to secure the calculated profit, but they do cause some emotional stress. In situations such as this I did my best to remain calm and understanding so we could arrive at an agreed price for the project.

The stress of trying to satisfy internal operations, your customer, the thought of losing the sale to a competitor and managing the project to produce good profits is part of being a salesperson. There are many times when you are willing to take a higher risk to close a sale while management wants to eliminate as much risk as possible by increasing the price. Other times management is fearful of risk to the point of walking away from some potentially good business along and losing the possibility of creating new business relationships. The larger the dollar figure of the project, the larger the amount of time spent in meetings with more stress for the salesperson. These stressful meetings to determine final pricing, specifications, terms and conditions of creating and presenting proposals and RFPs to customers is just the nature of the beast salespeople deal with. Try to stay as calm as possible and work through the give and take negotiations and it will work out one way or the other.

Remember the marketplace is huge and there are always more opportunities around the corner.

One way to handle the stress in dealing with the corporate machine is to always have an outside interest. It could be your church, social club like the Masons, Rotary, Elks, or the Lions, or hobbies like music, golf, snow skiing, hiking, mountain climbing, surfing, skin diving, gardening or whatever; something to give your mind a break from all those what's, if's, maybe's, could haves and should haves of selling.

The sales profession is one of the most stressful occupations. A salesperson is under the demands of the company to bring in the orders, develop new business, and manage the profitability of the sales. All these requirements to succeed along with having a social life dealing with partners, friends, and family can wear on a person. Once I observed a fellow salesperson having to deal with a divorce while at the same time trying to meet his sales goals. It was so emotionally stressful and difficult, he ended up leaving for a new occupation.

Early in my selling days I got so stressed that I had many sleepless nights pondering different business scenarios and outcomes. I have always felt that I was the provider in our family and no matter what, I was going to succeed and give my family the best possible life I could. In many ways I believe I accomplished that even with all the curve balls thrown at me during my life. Just keep trying to do the best you can. A positive attitude and a strong determination to succeed can take you a long way. Things will work out if you just smile and laugh at yourself when those difficult situations arise. There will always be peaks and valleys in our lives, but if you remain honest with yourself, look at situations from different points of view and be a little creative, usually things will turn out all right. As the saying goes: "when one door closes, another will open".

I spent almost all my career employed in sales with two of the largest multi-billion-dollar corporations (United Technologies and Lockheed Martin), surviving within their bureaucratic, ever-changing spider web structures. When asked how I survived, I jokingly would reply that you just need to be properly medicated.

An east coast upper management person visited our office once and casually said how people taking Prozac were so messed up. Little did he know that several people in our office who heard his comment were on some type of mood medication, possibly even Prozac. To handle stress a lot of people take to drinking alcohol and/or smoking pot. There is a thin line between using and abusing drugs. Many careers and lives have been destroyed by the overindulging in drugs. Some people have medical conditions and cannot partake in alcohol or pot. You may think that you are functioning fine while indulging, but sooner or later it will catch up with you. We had a manager in Las Vegas who became an alcoholic and one of our customers complained about his actions. He was removed from his management position and later terminated. Be careful, don't put your career or your loved ones on the line and lose your direction in life. If you are having trouble, ask for help!

A banker friend told me a few stockbrokers will be seen at the corner cocktail lounge knocking back a few before arriving at their offices in the morning. This type of existence is hard on your health and may possibly affect the ability to perform professionally. Alcohol and other drugs can destroy a person's ability to perform their occupation at a professional level. You need a clear mind so you can think on your feet while dealing with customers. If you smell of alcohol or pot around customers, they soon will be notifying your boss and/or looking for someone new to do business with.

Take vacations whenever possible. Vacations are there for a purpose, giving you some rest and relaxation from the daily grind. When you return you will be refreshed and more productive. Leave the laptop and the company smart phone at home with a message of when you will return and who will be responding to your customer's requests in your absence. If you take your job with you on vacation, then it is not a vacation. Men's Journal Magazine had an article titled: "The Too Weak Vacation" stating how in America we have the worst amount of time off than any other country and how the longer the vacation is the more productive workers are when they return. Some salespeople think that taking no vacations increases their value to upper management and shows how loyal they are by not taking any time off. That is not true -- management will just take advantage of you even more. Vacation is there for a purpose: rest and relaxation. Remember, happy workers make productive workers. Make sure that your customers are aware of your vacations and have a good plan in place for how they will be cared for during your absence. Make sure to cover all your bases prior to leaving on vacation, letting your manager know well in advance of when you are planning on leaving, how long you will be gone and who will be covering for you while you are on vacation. Your manager will appreciate being kept in the loop.

Life in general is stressful. Find your own way of dealing with it and you will be a much happier and successful person. Control your emotions by trying to stay calm. When you find yourself becoming stressed out, take a breather. Remove yourself from the situation for a time and regroup, and if you become emotionally stressful to a point that it starts affecting you physically and harming your relationships, get help. There is nothing wrong in asking for help, it is the smart thing to do! You can learn techniques in dealing with your emotions and stress, becoming a wiser person.

Life is too precious and too short to be miserable! Remember previously what George Harrison said: "All things will pass.". A week, a month, or a year down the road those tough situations that seemed so devastating at the time will have been resolved and have already floated down the river of time.

CHAPTER 49

Words of Wisdom

Having to deal with all the emotions of live along with the occupational happenings of a salesperson as when things start going sour and you need to perform damage control to remedy the problem(s), selling is still very gratifying. Income in the selling profession has a lot to do with what you sell. Someone selling hose and fittings probably will not be making the income of someone selling commercial real estate or Lear jets. Sales professionals still make the highest incomes.

In the beginning, Paul Allen and Bill Gates had to find a customer to sell their Microsoft products to so they could get their new company started. It was said that when they first met with IBM to present their new software products, IBM personnel would not even meet with them, leaving Paul and Bill in the lobby. But with persistence they prevailed, and history now tells their story. I have told many salespeople that if you don't get kicked out of at least three offices a day, you're not selling! This statement is symbolic, not factual. Meaning, you need to be persistent and do not get disappointed. If you knock on enough doors, sooner or later doors will start to open. Having the ability to handle rejection, letting disappointments roll off your back and move on is a good character trait to possess. Having to deal with operational people who can make your job miserable is part of the picture but being focused on your goals of closing good business usually will overcome those barriers placed in front of you.

Don't over analyze your customers. Sometimes it is best to be surprised and enjoy the learning experiences that your customers provide.

The feelings I get receiving a large order, a signed contract, or purchase order can be so rewarding that there were times when I would break into my happy dance in the office or on a city sidewalk.

We all make mistakes. Something you wish you never said or a decision you acted on that did not turn out the way you thought it would. A bad calculation causing a project to lose money. When you realize that you have made a mistake, you need to analyze it and learn from it. I screwed that one up big time, but I am never going to do that again! As I've touched on previously about making mistakes, if I learned from all my mistakes I should be a bloody genius by now! You can diffuse a bad situation quickly by just taking the blame for it. Jokingly I catch myself saying it's always the salesperson's fault. They sold it; therefore, it must be their fault. Even if it is not your fault, the problem or mistake can be diffused so everyone can put it behind them and move ahead to more current and important matters.

The fact remains that technology is always progressing. Due to the internet, people are becoming more introverted and not interacting with one another. People can purchase gasoline for their vehicles without the need of a cashier or buy items using Amazon and never leave their home. In China there are now restaurants without service personnel. You use an app on your smartphone to order your meal, pay for it and have it delivered by way of a programmed conveyor. With the use of facial recognition, there are now stores where you enter, take what you wish, and the purchase will be deducted from your debit card. The future will have fewer personal interactions. But in a business environment, there will always be transactions of providing products and services between a buyer and a salesperson. Personal inaction will still be required to close an agreement, capture a purchase order, or receive a signature on a contract.

When you have called on many customers, you end up meeting a lot of very interesting people and, if you are lucky enough, some of them may tell their personal stories. These experiences are priceless. A selling career can take you on travels across our country and beyond. You may end up visiting some of our great cities, dining at top restaurants, playing great golf courses and establish lifelong friendships. Your income might give you the ability to give your loved ones a comfortable home, travel experiences, and if you have children, you can provide them with a comfortable and caring life. Keep plugging away and good things will start to happen. Business will start coming your way. There is always a customer out there with a need for your products, you just need to go out there and find them. So, keep smiling with a positive attitude and you will soon start achieving your goals. As I have stated before, there will always be peaks and valleys in our lives, but if you persevere, the valleys become not so deep, and the peaks start having amazing views!

- Dr. Peter, "The Peter Principal"
- "Shut Up and Sell"

Personal note: If you ever find yourself in a conversation with a fellow employee or your manager and they happen to say, "it isn't personal, it's only business", be cautious! Business is personal - very personal. It is your livelihood, how you provide for your loved ones. If you feel you should correct the person making this dumb statement, do so. Some people make this statement, and it seems they are just revealing how out of touch they are. This statement is a crock of garbage.

CPSIA information can be obtained
at www.ICGtesting.com
Printed in the USA
BVHW041204240721
612638BV00011B/1316